"An eerily prescient play . . . blazes with an intensity that defines Kushner's best work." —MICHAEL KUCHWARA, AP

"Brilliant . . . this is a play for those who are interested in the root causes that preceded September 11, for those who can see through the fog of patriotism to the finer distinctions, who are finally ready to ask how on earth do we get out of this godforsaken place, who can bear to contemplate the thought that we have participated to some extent in our own tragedy." —JAMES RESTON, JR., *AMERICAN THEATRE*

"Kushner, a writer who is always on high alert to humanity as well as history, has, in the Homebody, created a character—an 'impassioned, fluttery, doomed' character—who is timeless as well as timely." —NANCY FRANKLIN, *NEW YORKER*

"*Homebody/Kabul* reminds you at a moment when such reminders are to be prized . . . how potent theater can be in asking the essential questions." —BEN BRANTLEY, SUNDAY *NEW YORK TIMES*

"*Homebody/Kabul* . . . is challenging, truthful, heroically humane. As he did in *Angels in America*, Kushner vivifies a theater of insight, at once precise and transcendent." —ADAM FELDMAN, BROADWAY.COM

"Dazzlingly eloquent." —CHARLES ISHERWOOD, *VARIETY*

"The issues of *Homebody/Kabul* may be complex and irresolvable, but the dramatic mission is not. It's as simple as Brecht's response to an interviewer who once asked him what theater should do: 'Try to discover the best way for people to live together,' he said. How many dramatists other than Tony Kushner would know how to begin to do that." —ELIZABETH POCHODA, *NATION*

"This is a haunting and beautiful play in spite of its author's best efforts to ruin it." —JOHN PODHORETZ *WEEKLY STANDARD*

D0167898

HOMEBODY/KABUL

Homebody/Kabul

TONY KUSHNER

WITH AN AFTERWORD
BY THE AUTHOR

THEATRE COMMUNICATIONS GROUP
NEW YORK

Homebody/Kabul is published by Theatre Communications Group, Inc., 355 Lexington Ave., New York, NY 10017-6603.

This publication is made possible in part with public funds from the New York State Council on the Arts, a State Agency.

TCG books are exclusively distributed to the book trade by Consortium Book Sales and Distribution, 1045 Westgate Dr., St. Paul, MN 55114.

LIBRARY OF CONGRESS CATALOGING-IN-PUBLICATION DATA
Kushner, Tony.
Homebody/Kabul / by Tony Kushner.—1st ed.
p. cm.
ISBN 1-55936-209-X
1. Kåbol (Afghanistan)—Drama. I. Title.

PS3561.U778 H66   2002
812'.54—dc21   2002020702

Book design and typography by Lisa Govan
Cover design by Susan Mitchell
Cover art "Mummy," mixed media, 2001 by Lesley Kushner
Cover photograph by Christian Carone

First edition, May 2002
Second printing, July 2002
Third printing, October 2002

For my dear friend Kika Markham,
who asked me for a monologue,
and in memory of my mother
Sylvia Deutscher Kushner

ACKNOWLEDGMENTS

It was very hard to write this play. I completed it only because many people helped me. I am profoundly indebted to them.

Most importantly, Nancy Hatch Dupree gave me her kind permission to use several sections and sentences from *An Historical Guide to Kabul,* altered to suit my purposes, in the Homebody's monologue. Ms. Dupree's elegant prose, dazzling erudition and deep love for her subject had a shaping effect not only on the style but also in the substance of *Homebody/Kabul.*

Another valuable collaborator, Nisar Ahmad Zuri, painstakingly translated my lines into Dari and Pashtun, and along the way provided me with invaluable information about Afghanistan. Mr. Zuri was a beacon and a delight, a joy to collaborate with and to learn from; I hope all his dreams come true.

Alan Edelstein introduced me to Mr. Zuri, and also shared with me his experiences in Kabul. I regret that we never managed to travel there together. I'm grateful to him and to Mike Hsu for introducing me to Alan.

At a rally in support of immigrants' rights, in London, in 1998, I met an Iraqi poet, Hussain al-Amily, who explained to me how he happened to learn Esperanto. His story inspired one aspect of the character of Khwaja Aziz Mondanabosh. I haven't been able to locate Mr. al-Amily to thank him; if he sees the play or reads this book, I hope it finds favor, and I hope he'll contact me.

Annie Castledine was the first director of the monologue, when it was part of a reading series sponsored by the
Moving Theater Company in London; Annie's shrewd enthu-
siasm for what seemed to me, at the moment of just having
written it, a strange bit of business, was incredibly helpful
and encouraging. Frances Alexander and the folks at the
Chelsea Centre Theatre in London gave the monologue its
first and second home.

The remarkable and brave Eve Ensler was similarly generous in sharing tales and photographs of her hair-raising
adventures in Afghanistan. Dr. Roger Walzman gave me hor-
rifying terminology to use in the dismemberment monologue. Benjamin Levy gave me a lovely explanation of electronic engineering which magically spoke to the heart of the
play. Madeleine George provided the Russian, James Magruder
the French, Carl Weber the German for Mahala. The Arabic
translations for Act Three, Scene 3 were provided by Munir
Metwally. Peter Marsden gave me useful information and
advice, and his book, *The Taliban*, one of the first on the subject, was my introduction to modern Afghan politics. Prof-
essor Deborah Stead improved my definition of recession.
Joseph Kamal made an important contribution to Doctor
Qari Shah's post-mortem which resulted in its final, ghastly
line; and Dylan Baker gave me permission to incorporate
into the script an inspired bit of business.

Craig Lucas, as ever, listened and held hands and dis-
pensed sterling dramaturgical advice. Michael Mayer gave
me some critical structural advice during previews, and was
in all ways as always my best girlfriend. Tony Taccone, a
honey of a man, committed Berkeley Rep to a production
many months ago, while he held an unproduceable 250-page
script in his hands. Joyce Ketay spent 275,943 hours on the
phone listening to me freak out and she never billed me for a
single minute.

Kimberly T. Flynn was busy during this production trying to save New York City from our pesticide-profligate mayor/

poisoner, but I drew endlessly from our years of exchanges, and I'm grateful as always for her great mind and spirit.

Dr. Deborah Glazer is a superb psychoanalyst. The play was written post-termination but its completion should be accounted the proof of the pudding.

My brother Eric, who always insists that I stop whining and get back to writing, held my feet to the fire on an all-important visit to Vienna, where he lives, and where the second and third acts of the play were begun, in the reading room of the Universität Wien. My sister Lesley, whose painting graces the cover of the book, also provided encouragement, advice, artistic and sororal commiseration, and love. We three, our father William, and my devoted Aunt Martha, know best and miss most the spirit that haunts the painting and the play.

Jim Nicola has been a dream of an artistic director, collaborator, buddy, dramaturg, producer, encourager since 1989, when *Millennium Approaches* had its first full reading in his theater. Without his insistence, openness, reckless faith, sharp eye, this play would never have been written.

Lynn Moffat and the staff and board of the Workshop all deserve medals, and all have my gratitude and love.

David Esbjornson and Beth Clancy helped me usher the play onto its first stage, the Chelsea Centre Theatre in London. I have no friends or collaborators whose talents and forbearance I treasure more. Declan Donnellan and Nick Ormerod sailed across the Atlantic to do the play at New York Theatre Workshop; I am grateful for their genius, their friendship and their spirit of adventure.

Linda Emond, a steadfast and encouraging friend and a wonderful actress, set new records for patient waiting while I groped about for the rest of the play.

Mandy Mishell Hackett has been a tireless and brilliant dramaturg, and her contribution to the development of *Homebody/Kabul* can only be described as central.

Mark Harris, my boyfriend/husband/partner/person, provided more indulgence, exhortation, admonishment, advice, than anyone else; as well as the name of the character Priscilla Ceiling and several truly remarkable insights which transformed the play.

Oskar Eustis, the dramaturgical voice I trust most in all the world, agreed to guide the play and the playwright through the straits and narrows; he is my navigator. His astonishing generosity and generous intellect and friendship make it possible to write. Long live the plumpes denken geschichtsline!

Homebody/Kabul premiered at New York Theatre Workshop (James C. Nicola, Artistic Director; Lynn Moffat, Managing Director) in New York City on December 19, 2001. It was directed by Declan Donnellan, with design by Nick Ormerod, lights by Brian MacDevitt, sound by Dan Moses Schreier, movement direction by Barbara Karger, dramaturgy by Oscar Eustis and Mandy Mishell Hackett, dialect coaching by Deborah Hecht and Gillian Lane-Plescia, cultural/language consulting by Nisar Ahmad Zuri, and production stage management by Martha Donaldson. The cast was as follows:

THE HOMEBODY	Linda Emond
DOCTOR QARI SHAH	Joseph Kamal
MULLAH AFTAR ALI DURRANNI	Firdous Bamji
MILTON CEILING	Dylan Baker
QUANGO TWISTLETON	Bill Camp
PRISCILLA CEILING	Kelly Hutchinson
LADY IN BURQA	Rita Wolf
A MUNKRAT	Dariush Kashani
KHWAJA AZIZ MONDANABOSH	Yusef Bulos
ZAI GARSHI	Sean T. Krishnan
MAHALA	Rita Wolf
THE MARABOUT	Sean T. Krishnan
A BORDER GUARD	Jay Charan

Homebody/Kabul opened at Trinity Repertory Company (Oskar Eustis, Artistic Director; Edgar Dobie, Managing Director) in Providence, Rhode Island, on March 15, 2002. It was directed by Oskar Eustis, with sets by Eugene Lee, lights by Deb Sullivan, sound by Peter Sasha Hurowitz, costumes by William Lane, dramaturgy by Oscar Eustis and Mandy Mishell Hackett, stage management by Jennifer Sturch and production stage management by Ruth E. Sternberg. The cast was as follows:

THE HOMEBODY	Anne Scurria
DOCTOR QARI SHAH	Demosthenes Chrysan
MULLAH AFTAR ALI DURRANNI	Donnie Keshawarz
MILTON CEILING	Brian McEleney
QUANGO TWISTLETON	Stephen Thorne
PRISCILLA CEILING	Angela Brazil
LADY IN BURQA	Yolande Bavan
A MUNKRAT	Omar Metwally
KHWAJA AZIZ MONDANABOSH	Apollo Dukakis
ZAI GARSHI	Deep Katdare
MAHALA	Yolande Bavan
THE MARABOUT	Omar Metwally
A BORDER GUARD	Omar Metwally

HOMEBODY/KABUL

CAST

THE HOMEBODY
British woman in her mid-forties.

DOCTOR QARI SHAH
Pashtun Afghan man in his forties/fifties, a doctor.

MULLAH AFTAR ALI DURRANNI
Pashtun Afghan man in his forties/fifties, Taliban minister.

MILTON CEILING
British man in his early forties, computer specialist,
husband of the Homebody.

QUANGO TWISTLETON
British man, early to mid-to-late thirties, aid worker,
unofficial liaison for the British government in Kabul.

PRISCILLA CEILING
British woman in her early twenties, unemployed, adrift,
daughter of Milton and the Homebody.

LADY IN BURQA

A MUNKRAT
Pashtun Afghan man, twenties, with the Nai Azz Munkar,
Taliban religious police.

KHWAJA AZIZ MONDANABOSH
Tajik Afghan man, fifties or sixties, a poet and guide-for-hire.

ZAI GARSHI
Afghan man, thirties or forties, a former actor, now sells hats.

MAHALA
Pashtun Afghan woman, thirties/forties,
before the Taliban arrived, a librarian.

THE MARABOUT
Afghan man, very old, a Sufi hermit.

A BORDER GUARD
Pashtun Afghan man, Taliban, twenties or thirties.

SETTING

The play takes place in London, England and Kabul, Afghanistan just before and just after the American bombardment of the suspected terrorist training camps in Khost, Afghanistan, August 1998.

The final scene, Periplum, is set in London in the spring of 1999.

NOTES

A Note for the Homebody:

When the Homebody, in Act One, Scene 1, refers to the street on which she found the hat shop, she doesn't mention its name; instead, where the name would fall in the sentence, she makes a wide, sweeping gesture in the air with her right hand, almost as if to say: "I know the name but I will not tell you." It is the same gesture each time.

The word "multiple-y" is pronounced multiplē.

In the Play:

A sentence ending with a ". . ." indicates that the speaker has trailed off . . .

A sentence ending with a "—" indicates that the speaker is interrupted by someone or something.

Among the many challenges regarding pronunciation presented by the script, it feels silly to make a special point of two in particular; nevertheless I feel compelled to note that the surname of Pelham Grenville Wodehouse (1881–1975) is pronounced "Woodhouse," and that Reuters is pronounced "Royters."

Zai Garshi *recites* Sinatra lyrics, the way one recites poetry; he shouldn't sing the lyrics.

Mahala's "projectile" on page 84 is the French word for "missile," and should be pronounced "projhecteel."

Act Three, Scene 1, works equally as well as the first scene of Act Three or the final scene of Act Two.

The shape of the map of present-day Afghanistan resembles a left-hand fist with the thumb open.

—NABI MISDAQ, *AHMAD SHAH DURRANI 1722–1772*

It is more appropriate to consider Afghanistan as a place of enormous complexity that has been subject to a constant state of flux throughout history rather than to view it as somehow caught in a time-warp, with life going on as it has always done.

—PETER MARSDEN, *THE TALIBAN*

Afghanistan lies at the crossroads of South and Central Asia; its northern plains an extension of the steppes to Turkmenistan, the Hindu Kush mountains an adjunct to the Himalayas, its southern deserts a prelude to the Persian Gulf. Linguistically, culturally and ethnically Afghanistan's northern Uzbeks, Turkmen and Tajiks look northwards to Central Asia, the centrally-located Hazaras look westwards to Iran, and the southern and eastern Pashtuns and Baluch find more resonance in the east in Pakistan. Although distinct from them, each group and region has more in common with its neighbors over the border than with each other.

—CHRIS BOWERS, "A BRIEF HISTORY OF AFGHANISTAN," FROM *ESSENTIAL FIELD GUIDE TO AFGHANISTAN*

"Periplum" is Pound's shorthand for a tour which takes you round then back again. And such a tour is by definition profitable, if not in coins then in knowledge.

—HUGH KENNER, *THE ELSEWHERE COMMUNITY*

These examples should teach you the way to treat hearts . . . The general technique consists in doing the opposite of everything the soul inclines to and craves. God (Exalted is He!) Has summed up all these things in His statement: "And whoever fears the standing before his Lord, and forbids his soul its whim, for him Heaven shall be the place of resort."

—AL-GHAZALI, *ON DISCIPLING THE SOUL AND BREAKING THE TWO DESIRES*

The world had been destroyed several times before the creation of man.

—LORD BYRON, *CAIN*

In Washington, Pentagon officials said that a U.S. warplane missed a Taliban military target at Kabul airport and that a 2,000 pound bomb the plane was carrying apparently struck a residential neighborhood.

At the scene of the hit, one man sat in his wheelchair, weeping next to a pile of rubble where his house once stood. Other residents wandered about in a daze.

"We lost everything, our house and property," one woman said. "We are so afraid of the attacks we have forgotten our own names and can't even understand what we say to each other."

—*NEW YORK TIMES*, OCTOBER 13, 2001

ACT ONE

SCENE I

A woman is sitting in a comfortable chair, in a pleasant room in her home in London. A table stands nearby, a lamp on the table. On the floor near her chair, a shopping bag. She is reading from a small book:

THE HOMEBODY
"Our story begins at the very dawn of history, circa 3,000 B.C. . . ."
(Interrupting herself:)
I am reading from an outdated guidebook about the city of Kabul. In Afghanistan. In the valleys of the Hindu Kush mountains. A guidebook to a city which as we all know, has . . . undergone change.
My reading, my research is moth-like. Impassioned, fluttery, doomed. A subject strikes my fancy: Kabul—you will see why, that's the tale I'm telling—but then, I can't help myself, it's almost perverse, in libraries, in secondhand bookshops, I invariably seek out not The Source but all that which was dropped by the wayside on the way to The Source, outdated guidebooks—this was published in 1965, and it is now 1998, so the book is a vestige superannuated by some . . . thirty-three years, long enough for Christ to have been born and die on the cross—old magazines, hysterical political treatises written by an advocate of some long-since defeated or abandoned or

9

transmuted cause; and I find these irrelevant and irresistible, ghostly, dreamy, the knowing what *was* known before the more that has since become known overwhelms . . . As we are, many of us, overwhelmed, and succumbing to luxury . . .

(She reads from the guidebook:)

"Our story begins at the very dawn of history, circa 3,000 B.C., when the Aryans, not in armies but in family groups, traveled south from beyond the River Oxus, to cross the Hindu Kush mountains on their way to northern India. This crossing must have made a great impression for, nearly two thousand years later, when the Rigveda, the great hymnic epic poem of the Aryan peoples, is written down, several verses retain the memory of the serene beauty of the valleys of the Kabul River."

(She looks up from the guidebook)

Several months ago I was feeling low and decided to throw a party and a party needs festive hats. So I took the tube to _____, *(She gestures; see prefatory "Notes" above)* where there are shops full of merchandise from exotic locales, wonderful things made by people who believe, as I do not, as *we* do not, in magic; or who used to believe in magic, and not so long ago, whose grandparents believed in magic, believed that some combination of piety, joy, ecstasy, industry, brought to bear on the proper raw materials, wood for instance known to be the favored nesting place of a certain animus or anima possessed of powers released, enlisted in beneficent ways towards beneficent ends when carved, adorned, adored just so . . . Before colonization and the savage stripping away of such beliefs. For magic beliefs are immensely strong, I think, only if their essential fragility is respected. It's a paradox. If such beliefs, magic beliefs, are untouched, they endure. And who knows? Work magic, perhaps. If they are untouched; and that is hard, for such is the expansive nature of these times that every animate and inanimate thing, corporeal or incorporeal, actual or ideational, real or imagined, every, every discrete unit of . . . of *being*: if

a thing can be said to *be*, to *exist*, then such is the nature of these expansive times that this thing which is must suffer to be *touched*. Ours is a time of connection; the private, and we must accept this, and it's a hard thing to accept, the private is *gone*. All must be touched. All touch corrupts. All must be corrupted. And if you're thinking how awful these sentiments are, you are perfectly correct, these are awful times, but you must remember as well that *this* has always been the chiefest characteristic of The Present, to everyone living through it; always, throughout history, and so far as I can see for all the days and years to come until the sun and the stars fall down and the clocks have all ground themselves to expiry and the future has long long shaded away into Time Immemorial: The Present is *always* an awful place to be. And it remains awful to us, the scene of our crime, the place of our shame, for at least Oh, let's say three full decades of recession—by which word, recession, I am to be taken to mean recedence, not recession as in two consecutive quarters of negative growth in gross domestic product. For a three-decades regnum of imperceptible but mercifully implacable recedency we shudder to recall the times through which we have lived, the Recent Past, about which no one wants to think; and then, have you noticed? Even the most notorious decade three or four decades later is illumined from within. Some light inside is switched on. The scenery becomes translucent, beautifully lit; features of the landscape glow; the shadows are full of agreeable color. Cynics will attribute this transformation to senescence and nostalgia; I who am optimistic, have you noticed? attribute this inner illumination to understanding. It is wisdom's hand which switches on the light within. Ah, now I see what that was all about. Ah, now, now I see why we suffered so back then, now I see what we went through. I understand.
(She reads from the guidebook:)
"Nothing is known of the Aryan passage through the valleys of the Hindu Kush, no writing or significant structure

remains from the Aryan settlements which undoubtedly existed on the banks of the Kabul River, one of which would eventually grow into the city of Kabul. The first contemporaneous account to mention the city is recorded circa 520 B.C., when Darius the Great, Achaemenid Persian conqueror and builder of Persepolis, annexed twenty-nine countries to the Persian empire, parts of India, all of what we now know as Afghanistan, including the Kabul Valley. In the summer of 329 B.C., Alexander the Macedonian, having trampled the Achaemenid imperium in his victorious march through Persia, makes camp in the Hindu Kush city of Khandahar, and orders the building of the city of Alexandria-ad-Caucasum."

(She looks up from the guidebook)

Oh I love the world! I love love love love the world! Having said so much, may I assume most of you will have dismissed me as a simpleton? I cannot hope to contravene your peremptory low estimation, which may for all its peremptoriness nevertheless be exactly appropriate. I live with the world's mild censure, or would do were it the case that I ever strayed far enough from my modesty, or should I say my essential surfeit of inconsequence, to so far attract the world's attention as to provoke from it its mild censure; but I have never strayed so far from the unlit to the spotlight, and so should say rather that I live with the world's utter indifference, which I have always taken to be a form of censure-in-potentia.

I speak . . . I can't help myself. Elliptically. Discursively. I've read too many books, and that's not boasting, for I haven't read *many* books, but I've read too many, exceeding I think my capacity for syncresis—is that a word?—straying rather into synchisis, which is a word. So my diction, my syntax, well, it's so *irritating*, I apologize, I do, it's very hard, I know. To listen. I blame it on the books, how else to explain it? My parents don't speak like this; no one I know does; no one does. It's an *alien influence*, and my borders have only ever been broached by books. Sad to say.

Only ever been broached by books. Except once, briefly. Which is I suppose the tale I'm telling, or rather, trying to tell.

You must be patient. There is an old Afghan saying, which, in rough translation from the Farsi, goes: *"The man who has patience has roses. The man who has no patience has no trousers."* I am not fluent in Farsi, of course, I read this, and as I say it must be a rough translation.

(She reads from the guidebook:)

"Alexander the Great summoned to the Kabul Valley a mighty army comprising tens of thousands of soldiers from Egypt, Persia and Central Asia and went on to conquer India. When Alexander's own troops grew weary of battle, in 325 B.C., they forced their commander to desist from further conquest. Alexander died in 323 B.C., just as he was planning a return to the Hindu Kush to oversee the Grecianization of this most remarkable land."

(She pauses her reading)

My husband cannot bear my . . . the sound of me and has threatened to leave on this account and so I rarely speak to him anymore. We both take powerful antidepressants. His pills have one name and mine another. I frequently take his pills instead of mine so I can know what he's feeling. I keep mine in a glass bowl next to the bathroom sink, a nice wide-mouthed bowl, very wide, wide open, like an epergne, but so far as I know he never takes my pills but ingests only his own, which are yellow and red, while mine are green and creamy-white; and I find his refusal to sample dull. A little dull.

(She resumes, from the guidebook:)

"By 322 B.C., only a year after Alexander's death, his vast Macedonian empire had disassembled. Herodotus tells us that the hill tribes of the Kabul Valley were among the first and the most ferocious in rejecting Macedonian authority. Seleucus Nicator, Alexander's successor in the east, attempted to regain the Hindu Kush but was daunted when he encountered, in 305 B.C., in the passes of the Hindu Kush, the armed

forces of the Maurya Dynasty which had come to rule India. In exchange for the hand of the daughter of the Maurya emperor, Chandragupta, and for five hundred elephants, the Kabul Valley passed for the first time under Indian suzerainty."
(She puts the guidebook down)
A party needs hats. I had no hope that this would be a good party. My parties are never good parties. This party was intended to celebrate my husband's having completed some joyless task at his place of business, which has something to do with the routing of multiple-y expressive electronic tone signals at extraordinary speeds across millions upon millions of kilometers of wire and cable and fiber and space; I understand none of it and indeed it's quite impossible imagining my husband having to do in any real way with processes so . . . speedy, myriad, nervous, miraculous. But that parti-colored cloud of gas there, in that galaxy there so far away, that cloud there so hot and blistered by clustering stars, exhaling protean scads of infinitely irreducible fiery data in the form of energy pulses and streams of slicing, shearing, unseeable light—does that nebula know it nebulates? Most likely not. So my husband. It knows nothing, its *nature* is to stellate and constellate and nebulate and add its heft and vortices and frequencies to the Universal Drift, un-self-consciously effusing, effusing, gaseously effusing, and so my husband, and so not I, who seem forever to be imploding and collapsing and am incapable it would seem of lending even this simple tale to the Universal Drift, of telling this simple tale without supersaturating my narrative with maddeningly infuriating or more probably irritating synchitic expegeses.
Synchitic expegeses. Jesus.
A party needs hats and in my mind's eye I remembered quite remarkable hats, not as tall as fezzes nor yet as closely cleaving to the curve of the skull as a skullcap, but really rather pillboxy as ladies wore hats in the early '60s; but these mind's-eye hats were made of tough brilliant dyed wools and scraps of elaborate geometrically arabesqued carpet into

which sequins and diamantines and carbuncles and glassene beading had been sewn to dazzling, charming premodern effect. I could see these hats perched on top of the heads of the family members and friends who usually appear at my parties, lovely lovely people all of them but when we assemble we rather . . . affect one another, one might even say *afflict* one another, in baleful ways and tend to dampen one another's festive spirits, there's no . . . I suppose one would like something combustible at a party, something catalytic, some fizz, each element triggering transformation in all the other elements till all elements, which is to say, *guests*, are . . . surprising to themselves and return home feeling less . . . less certain of . . . those certainties which . . . *Because* of which, for example, powerful antidepressants are consumed.

(She reads from the guidebook:)

"The third century B.C. was a prosperous time for the Kabul Valley, situated midway between the empires of the Seleucids and the Mauryas, profiting thusly from an extensive trade with both which must have included furs from Central Asia and a recent discovery of the Chinese, silk. By the end of the third century the far-flung Mauryan empire had disappeared and a period of disorder, migration and tribal unrest follows, for which the records are clouded and confused."

(She looks up from the guidebook)

My antidepressant is called . . . something, a made-up word, a portmanteau chemical cocktail word confected by punning psychopharmacologists but I can never remember precisely what to ask for when I . . . My husband explains to me with bitter impacted patience each time I request it of him the workings of . . . Ameliorate-za-pozulac, its workings upon my brain; I cannot retain his bitter impacted explanation, but I believe it's all to do with salt somehow. I believe in fact this drug is a kind of talented salt. And so I imagine my brain floating in a salt bath, frosted with a rime of salt, a pickle-brine brain, pink-beige walnut-wrinkled nutmeat within a crystalliform quartzoid ice-white hoarfrost casing, a gemmy shell, gemmiparous: budding. How any of this is meant to counteract depression is more than I can say.

Perhaps it is the sufficient pleasing image which cheers one and makes life's burdens less difficult to bear.

(She reads from the guidebook:)

"In the middle of the second century B.C., during the Greco-Bactrian confusion, a Chinese tribe, the Hsiung-Nu, attacked a rival tribe, the Yueh-Chih, and drove them from their homes to what is now southern Afghanistan. Then the Hsiung-Nu, displaced from their new homes by another Chinese tribe, also migrated to Afghanistan and once again displaced the Yueh-Chih, who emigrated to the Kabul Valley. As the first century B.C. dawns, the Valley, populated by Indo-Greeks, Mauryas and Macedonians, is now surrounded by the restless nomadic kingdoms of the Yueh-Chih.

"By 48 B.C. the Chinese tribes are united under the banner of their largest clan, the Kushans. From the city of Kapisa, the Kushan court came to rival the Caesars in Rome." And I'd never *heard* of the Kushans, have you? Nor for that matter the Greco-Bactrian Confusion! Though it *feels* familiar, does it not, the Greco-Bactrian Confusion? When did it end? The guidebook does not relate. *Did* it end? Are we perhaps still in it? Still *in* the Greco-Bactrian Confusion? Would it surprise you, really, to learn that we are? Don't you feel it would I don't know *explain* certain things? "Ah yes it is hard I know, to *understand* but you see it's the Greco-Bactrian Confusion, which no one ever actually bothered clearing up, and, well here we are."

But let us return to the Kushans:

"From the city of Kapisa, the Kushan court came to rival the Caesars in Rome. Buddhism, Hinduism, Grecian and Persian deities are gathered into the valleys of the Hindu Kush where a remarkable cross-fertilization takes place."

(She puts the guidebook down)

In my mind's eye, yet from memory: I had seen these abbreviated fezlike pillboxy attenuated yarmulkite millinarisms, um, *hats*, I'm sorry I *will* try to stop, *hats*, yes, in a crowded shop on _____ *(Gesture)* which I must have passed and mentally noted on my way towards God knows what, who cares, a dusty shop crowded with artifacts, relics, remnants, little . . . doodahs of a culture once aswarm with spirit matter, radiant with potent magic the disenchanted dull detritus of which has washed up upon our culpable shores, its magic now shriveled into the safe container of *aesthetic*, which is to say, *consumer* appeal. You know, Third World junk. As I remember, as my mind's eye saw, through its salt crust, Afghan junk. That which was once Afghan, which we, having waved our credit cards in its general direction, have made into junk. I remembered the shop, where I thought it was, what its windows were like, sure I'd never find it again and yet there it was in my mind's eye and I traveled to the spot my mind's eye had fixed upon and I was correct! Took the tube, chewed my nails, there was the shop! Precisely as my salt-wounded mind's eye's corneal rotogravured sorry sorry. I found the shop. It was run by Afghan refugees.

And here are the hats. There are ten. They cost three ninety-nine each.

(She displays the hats, removing them one by one from the shopping bag and putting them on the table)

Looking at the hat we imagine not bygone days of magic belief but the suffering behind the craft, this century has taught us to direct our imagination however fleetingly toward the hidden suffering: evil consequence of evil action taken long ago, conjoining with relatively recent wickedness and wickedness perpetuated now, in August 1998, now now now even as I speak and speak and speak . . . But whether the product of starveling-manned sweatshop or remote not-on-the-grid village, poor yet still resisting the onslaught of modernity, touched, of course, yet not, though it is only a matter of time, isn't it? not corrupted; whether removed from the maker by the middleman to the merchant by filch or swindle or gunpoint or even murder; whether, for that

matter, even Afghan in origin; and not Pakistani; or
Peruvian; if not in point of fact made in London by children,
aunts and elderly uncles in the third-floor flat above the shop
on _____ *(Gesture)*: the hats are beautiful; relatively
inexpensive; sinister if you've a mind to see them that way;
and sad. As dislocations are. And marvelous, as dislocations
are. Always bloody.
This one is particularly nice.
(She puts a hat on her head, and reads from the guidebook:)
"Severe economic crises throughout the region in the second
century A.D. made it easy for the Sassanians, a purely Iranian
Persian dynasty, to claim the Hindu Kush Valley as a semi-
independent satrapy. The inhabitants of Kabul from the
Kushano-Sassanian period appear to have remained
Buddhist, while their Sassanian overlords were obstreperous
worshipers of Zoroaster." *(She looks up from the book)*
"Obstreperous worshipers of Zoroaster"! For that phrase
alone I deem this book a worthy addition to my pickpenny
library of remaindered antilegomenoi. *(Back to the book)*
"Sassanian hegemony—" *(Up from the book)* Antilegomenoi
are volumes of castoff or forgotten knowledge, in case you
were wondering. *(Back to the book)* "Sassanian hegemony
was toppled by the Hephthalites, or white Huns, who commenced a reign of legendary destructiveness around 400 A.D.,
savagely persecuting the indigenous worship of Buddha—
Buddhism having found many adherents among Hindu
Kush peoples as its monks carried news of the Buddha
from India through Afghanistan to China. Apart from their
fabled viciousness, almost nothing is known about the
Hephthalites."
(She looks up from the guidebook)
Nothing when this book was written, and it is rather old.
Perhaps more is known now though archaeology in the area
has been interrupted. Very little digging, except recently, did
you read this, the bodies of two thousand Taliban soldiers
were found in a mass grave in northern Afghanistan, prison-

ers who were executed, apparently by soldiers loyal to the overthrown government of Burhanuddin Rabbani. So someone is digging, and perhaps more now is known about the Hephthalites.

(She reads from the guidebook:)

"Hephthalite rule ended in 531 A.D. after which a state of anarchy prevailed over the entire region, each town protected by an independent chieftain, and the remaining Hephthalite princes"—who, you will remember, made their appearance just one paragraph previous, razing Buddhist temples—"the remaining Hephthalite princes having by this time *converted to Buddhism.*"

And made a great vulgar noise about it, I shouldn't wonder. I find myself disliking intensely the Hepthalites.

"Meanwhile, in 642, the banner of Islam"—Islam at last!—"carried forth from the deserts of Arabia, halted its eastern progress when its armies tried to penetrate the heart of what is now Afghanistan; for every hill and town was defended by fierce tribal warriors. Several hundred years were to pass before Kabul would fully surrender to Islam."

(Turning pages, summarizing:)

This brings us to the end of the millennium, 1023. Kabul over the next three or four hundred years will be conquered by first this empire builder and then that one. Genghis Khan swam through the area on a river of blood. The Great Tamurlaine, a Timurid, wounded his foot during a battle near Kabul, says the guidebook, and whatever it was he was named before (the book is not helpful on this) he was henceforth and forevermore known as Timur-I-Lang, Timur Who Limps. Timur-I-Lang, Tamurlaine. Kabul re-baptised him.

(She puts the guidebook down)

And this is what happened, and it's all there is to my little tale, really: the hats were in a barrel which could be seen through the window; puppets hung from the ceiling, carved freestanding figurines, demiurges, attributes, symbols, carven abstractions representing metaphysical principles criti-

cal to the governance of perfect cosmologies now lost to all
or almost all human memory; amber beads big as your
baby's fists, armor plates like pangolin scales strung on thick
ropey catgut cordage meant to be worn by rather large
rather ferocious men, one would imagine, or who knows;
hideous masks with great tusks and lolling tongues and
more eyes than are usual, mind's eyes I suppose and revolv-
ing wire racks filled with postcards depicting the severed
heads of The Queen and Tony Blair, well not *severed* neces-
sarily but with no body appended; Glaswegian *A to Zed
Guides* and newspapers in Arabic, in Urdu, in Pushtu, video-
cassettes of rock balladeers from Benares: well why go on
and on, sorry I'm sorry, we've all been in these sorts of shops,
no bigger than from here to there, haven't we? As if a many-
cameled caravan, having roamed across the entire postcolo-
nial not-yet-developed world, crossing the borders of the
rainforested kingdoms of Kwashiorkor and Rickets and
Untreated Gum Disease and High Infant Mortality Rates,
gathering with desperate indiscriminateness—is that the
word?—on the mudpitted unpaved trade route its bits and
boodle, had finally beached its great heavy no longer
portable self in a narrow coal-scuttle of a shop on
_____ *(Gesture), here,* here, caravanseraied here, in the
developed and overdeveloped and over-overdeveloped paved
wasted now deliquescent post-First World postmodern city
of London; all the camels having flopped and toppled and
fallen here and died of exhaustion, of shock, of the heartache
of refugees, the goods simply piled high upon their drome-
dary bones, just where they came to rest, and set up shop
atop the carcasses, and so on.
I select ten hats, thread my way through the musty heaps of
swag and thrownaway and offcast and godforsaken sorry
sorry through the merchandise to the counter where a man,
an Afghan man, my age I think, perhaps a bit older, stands
smiling eager to ring up my purchases and make an imprint
of my credit card, and as I hand the card to him I see that

three fingers on his right hand have been hacked off, following the line of a perfect clean diagonal from middle to ring to
little finger, which, the last of the three fingers in the diagonal cut's descent, by, um, hatchet blade? was hewn off almost
completely—like this, you see?
(She demonstrates)
But a clean line, you see, not an accident, a measured surgi-
cal cut, but not surgery as we know it for what possible
medicinal purpose might be served? I tried, as one does, not
to register shock, or morbid fascination, as one does my eyes
unfocused my senses fled startled to the roof of my skull and
then off into the ether like a rapid vapor indifferent to the
obstacle of my cranium WHOOSH, clean slate, tabula rasa,
terra incognita, where am I yet still my mind's eye somehow
continuing to record and detail that poor ruined hand slip-
ping my MasterCard into the . . . you know, that thing, that
roller press thing which is used to . . . Never mind. Here, in
London, that poor ruined hand.
Imagine.
I know nothing of this hand, its history, of course, nothing.
I did know, well I have learnt since through research that
Kabul, which is the ancient capital of Afghanistan, and
where once the summer pavilion of Amir Abdur Rahman
stood shaded beneath two splendid old chinar trees, beloved
of the Moghuls, Kabul, substantial portions of which are
now great heaps of rubble, was it was claimed by the Moghul
Emperor Babur founded by none other than Cain himself.
Biblical Cain. Who is said to be buried in Kabul, in the gar-
dens south of Bala-Hissar in the cemetery known as
Shohada-I-Salehin.
I should like to see that. The Grave of Cain. Murder's Grave.
Would you eat a potato plucked from *that* soil?
(She reads from the guidebook:)
"The mighty Moghul emperors, who came to rule the Hindu
Kush and all of India, adored Kabul and magnified and
exalted it. By the eighteenth century the Moghuls, ruling

from Delhi and Agra, succumbed to luxury"—that's what it says, they succumbed to luxury. "Modern Afghanistan is born when, in 1747, heretofore warring Afghan tribal chiefs forge for themselves a state, proclaiming Ahmed Shah Durrani, age twenty-five, King of the Afghans."

(She looks up from the guidebook)

And so the Great Game begins. The Russians seize Khazakstan, the British seize India, Persia caves in to the Russians, the first Anglo-Afghan war is fought, the bazaar in Kabul is burnt and many many people die, Russia seizes Bokhara, the second Anglo-Afghan war, the First World War, the October Revolution, the third Anglo-Afghan war, also known as the Afghanistan War of Independence, Afghanistan sovereignty first recognized by the Soviet Union in 1921, followed by aid received from the Soviet Union, followed by much of the rest of the twentieth century, Afghanistan is armed by the U.S.S.R. against the Pakistanis, the U.S. refuses assistance, militant Islamic movements form the seed of what will become the Mujahideen, the U.S. begins sending money, much civil strife, approaching at times a state of civil war, over liberal reforms such as the unveiling of and equal rights for women, democratic elections held, martial law imposed, the Soviet Union invades, the Mujahideen are armed, at first insufficiently, then rather handsomely by the U.S., staggering amounts of firepower, some captured from the Soviets, some purchased, some given by the West, missiles and antiaircraft cannon and etc. etc., the Soviets for ten years do their best to outdo the Hephthalites in savagery, in barbarism, then like so many other empires traversing the Hindu Kush the U.S.S.R. is swept away, and now the Taliban, and . . .

Well.

(She closes the guidebook and puts it down)

Afghanistan is one of the poorest countries in the world. With one of the world's most decimated infrastructures. No tourism. Who in the world would wish to travel there? In Afghanistan today I would be shrouded entirely in a *burqa*, I should be subject to *hejab*, I should live in terror of the *sharia hudud*, or more probably dead, unregenerate chatterer that I am.

While I am signing the credit card receipt I realize all of a sudden I am able to speak perfect Pushtu, and I ask the man, who I now notice is very beautiful, not on account of regularity of features or smoothness of the skin, no, his skin is broken by webs of lines inscribed by hardships, siroccos and strife, battle scars, perhaps, well certainly the marks of some battle, some life unimaginably more difficult than my own; I ask him to tell me what had happened to his hand. And he says: I was with the Mujahideen, and the Russians did this. I was with the Mujahideen, and an enemy faction of Mujahideen did this. I was with the Russians, I was known to have assisted the Russians, I did informer's work for Babrak Karmal, my name is in the files if they haven't been destroyed, the names I gave are in the files, there are no more files, I stole bread for my starving family, I stole bread *from* a starving family, I profaned, betrayed, according to some stricture I erred and they chopped off the fingers of my hand. *Look, look at my country, look at my Kabul, my city, what is left of my city? The streets are as bare as the mountains now, the buildings are as ragged as mountains and as bare and empty of life, there is no life here only fear, we do not live in the buildings now, we live in terror in the cellars in the caves in the mountains, only God can save us now, only order can save us now, only God's Law harsh and strictly administered can save us now, only The Department for the Promotion of Virtue and the Prevention of Vice can save us now, only terror can save us from ruin, only neverending war, save us from terror and neverending war, save my wife they are stoning my wife, they are chasing her with sticks, save my wife save my daughter from punishment by God, save us from God, from war, from exile, from oil exploration, from no oil exploration, from the West, from the children with rifles, carrying stones, only children with rifles, carrying stones, can save us now.* You will never understand. It is hard, it was hard work to get into the U.K. I am happy

here in the U.K. I am terrified I will be made to leave the
U.K. I cannot wait to leave the U.K. I despise the U.K. I voted
for John Major. I voted for Tony Blair. I did not, I cannot
vote, I do not believe in voting, the people who ruined my
hand were right to do so, they were wrong to do so, my hand
is most certainly ruined, *you will never understand,* why are
you buying so many hats?
(Little pause)
We all romp about, grieving, wondering, but with rare excep-
tion we mostly remain suspended in the Rhetorical Colloidal
Forever that agglutinates between Might and Do. "Might do,
might do." I have a friend who says that. "Off to the cinema,
care to come?" "Might do." "Would you eat a potato plucked
from that soil?" "Might do." Jesus wants you hot or cold but
she will hedge her every bet, and why should she not? What
has this century taught the civilized if not contempt for those
who merely contemplate; the lockup and the lethal injection
for those who Do. Awful times, as I have said, our individual
degrees of culpability for said awfulness being entirely
bound-up in our correspondent degrees of action, malevolent or not, or in our correspondent degrees of inertia, which
can be taken as a form of malevolent action if you've a mind
to see it that way. I do. I've such a mind. My husband . . .
Never mind. We shall most of us be adjudged guilty when we
are summoned before the Judgment Seat. But guilt?
Personal guilt? *(Wringing hands)* Oh, oh . . . No more morally
useful or impressive than adult nappy rash, and nearly as
unsightly, and ought to be kept as private, ought guilt, as any
other useless unimpressive unsightly inflammation. Not suit-
able for public exchange. And all conversation such as we
are having, and though you've said nothing whatsoever we
are still conversing, I think, since what I say is driven by fear
of you, sitting there before me, by absolute terror of your
censure and disdain, and so you need say nothing, you
would only weaken your position, whatever it may be, whatever you may be making of this, by speaking, I mean, look at

me, look at what I am doing, to myself, to what you must think of me, if ever you chance upon me on _____ *(Gesture)*, out shopping, what will you think? Avoid! Her! All conversation constitutes public exchange was my point, and there are rules of engagement, and skin rash should be displayed in public only for medicinal restorative purposes, inviting the healing rays of the sun and the drying authority of the fresh crisp breeze, and not for the garnering of admiration and the harvesting of sympathy. For most of us deserve neither, and I include myself in that harsh judgment, no matter how guilty we are or feel ourselves to be, my optimism notwithstanding.

I watch as he puts the ten hats in a carrier-bag and feel no surprise when he informs someone in the back of the shop, in Pushto, in which language as I mentioned I now find myself fluent, he's taking the rest of the afternoon off, and he offers me his right hand. I take it and we go out of the shop but no longer on _____ *(Gesture)*, we are standing on a road, a road in Kabul. I hold on tight to his ruined right hand, and he leads me on a guided tour through his city. There are the mountains, unreal as clouds; it is shamelessly sweet, the wreckage rack and ruination all there of course, it's ineffaceable now, this holocaustal effacement, but the gardens of Babur Shah are there too, just like the outdated guidebook promises, and the room in which handsome Shah Shujah, about thirty years of age, of olive complexion and thick black beard, puppet monarch of the British Mission, detested and soon to be murdered by his own insurgent people, displays himself to breathtaking effect, his visitors imagining him at first to be dressed in an armor of jewels, how impractical *that* would be, but actually he wears a green tunic over which are worked flowers of gold and a breast plate of diamonds, shaped like flattened fleurs-de-lis, ornaments of the same kind on each thigh, emeralds above the elbows, diamonds on each wrist, strings of pearls like cross belts but loose, a crown not encrusted with jewels but apparently entirely formed of those precious materials, the whole so complicated and dazzling it is difficult to understand and impossible to describe, and the throne is covered with a cloth adorned with pearls . . .

(She cries softly)

And the scent of the hat merchant takes me by surprise, toasted almonds, and he smiles a broader shy smile which shatters his face into a thousand shards and near a place called Bemaru, thought to be the grave of Bibi Mahru, the Moon-Faced Lady, who died of grief when her betrothed was reported slain on the battlefield, but he wasn't slain, he'd only lost his hand, near her grave, visited by mothers with ailing children, even today, *especially today* when there are many many such cases, many ailing children—demurely hidden from the sight of the ailing and the destitute and war-ravaged we, the hat merchant and I, make love beneath a chinar tree, which is it is my guess a kind of plane tree, beloved of the Moghuls. We kiss, his breath is very bitter, he places his hand inside me, it seems to me his whole hand inside me, and it seems to me a whole hand. And there are flocks of pigeons the nearby villagers keep banded with bronze rings about their legs, and they are released each afternoon for flight, and there is frequently, in the warmer months, kite flying to be seen on the heights of Bemaru.

(Pause)

I sign the receipt, I have paid, he hands me the carrier-bag stuffed with my purchase and with his smile indicates we are done and I should depart. And a chill wind blows up my bones and I long to be back in the safety of my kitchen and I leave the shop pondering the possibility that my prescribed dosage of . . . Mealy-aza-opzamene is too strong, or that sampling my husband's pills . . . perhaps these two chemicals are immiscible.

And yes in fact I do have children, well, *one*. A child. For whom alas nothing ever seems to go well. The older she gets. My fault entirely I'm sure or at least so I am told by my husband the near-mute purveyor of reproachful lids-lowered glances. But this is neither here nor there. We all loved one another, once, but today it simply isn't so or isn't what it used to be, it's . . . well, love.

I love the world. I know how that sounds, inexcusable and vague, but it's all I can say for myself, I love the world, really I do . . . *Love*. Not the vast and unembraceable and orbicular world, this is no gigantine rhapsodic—for all that one might suspect a person who uses words like gigantine—God!—of narcissism, my love is not that overstretched self-aggrandizing hyperinflated sort of adulation which seeks in the outsized and the impossible-to-clearly-comprehend a reflection commensurate with its own oceanic . . . of, well, I suppose of the extent to which the soul excuse me I mean the self is always an insoluble mystery to the narcissist who flatters herself that feeling of vagueness always hanging about her which not a salt in the world can cure is something grand, oceanic, titanically erotic while of course what it really is is nothing more than an inadequately shaped unsteady incoherent . . . quoggy sort of bubble where the solid core ought to be.

I love . . . this guidebook. Its foxed unfingered pages, forgotten words: "Quizilbash." Its sorrowing supercessional displacement by all that has since occurred. So lost; and also so familiar. The home *(She makes the gesture)* away from home. *Recognizable*: not how vast but how *crowded* the world is, consequences to *everything*: the Macedonians, marching east; one tribe displacing another; or one moment in which the heart strays from itself and love is . . . gone?

What after all is a child but the history of all that has befallen her, a succession of displacements, bloody, beautiful? How could any mother not love the world? What else is love but recognition? Love's nothing to do with happiness. Power has to do with happiness. Love has only to do with home.

(Little pause)

Where stands the homebody, safe in her kitchen, on her culpable shore, suffering uselessly watching others perishing in the sea, wringing her plump little maternal hands, oh, oh. Never *joining* the drowning. Her feet, neither rooted nor moving. The ocean is deep and cold and erasing. But how dreadful, really unpardonable, to remain dry.

Look at her, look at her, she is so unforgivably dry. Neither here nor there. She does not drown, she . . . succumbs. To Luxury. She sinks. Terror-struck, down, down into . . . um, the dangerous silent spaces, or rather places, with gravity and ground, down into the terrible silent gardens of the private, in the frightening echoing silence of which a grieving voice might be heard, chattering away, keening, rocking, shrouded, trying to express that which she lacks all power to express but which she knows must be expressed or else . . . death. And she would sound I suppose rather like what I sound like now:

(Whispers:)

Avoid! Her!

And now my daughter. Come home as one does. She must have and may not budge, and I understand, I am her mother, she is . . . starving. I . . . withhold my touch.

The touch which does not understand is the touch which corrupts, the touch which does not understand that which it touches is the touch which corrupts that which it touches, and which corrupts itself.

And so yes, when unexpectedly a curtain I'd not noticed before is parted by a ruined hand, which then beckons, I find myself improbably considering . . .

(Pause)

The hats at the party are a brilliant success. My guests adore them. They are hard to keep on the head, made for smaller people than the people we are and so they slip off, which generates amusement, and the guests exchange them while dancing, kaleidoscopic and self-effacing and I think perhaps to our surprise in some small way meltingly intimate, someone else's hat atop your head, making your scalp stiffen at the imagined strangeness; and to a select group in the kitchen

I tell about the merchant who sold them to me, and a friend wisely asks, how do you even know he's Afghan, and of course that's a good question, and the fact is I don't. And I wonder for an instant that I didn't ask. "Would you make love to a stranger with a mutilated hand if the opportunity was offered you?" "Might do," she says. Frank Sinatra is playing: such an awful awful man, such perfect perfect music! A paradox!
(Frank Sinatra starts to sing "It's Nice to Go Trav'ling." She sings the first two verses with him, putting the hats back in the shopping bag, one by one:)

It's very nice to go trav'ling
To Paris, London and Rome
It's oh so nice to go trav'ling,
But it's so much nicer yes it's so much nicer
To come home.
It's very nice to just wander
The camel route to Iraq,
It's oh so nice to just wander
But it's so much nicer yes it's oh so nice
To wander back . . .

(The music fades. The Homebody stands, takes the coat draped over the back of the empty chair, and puts it on. Buttoning the coat, she says:)

In the seventeenth century the Persian poet Sa'ib-I-Tabrizi was summoned to the court of the Moghul emperors in Agra, and on his way he passed, as one does, Kabul, the city in the Hindu Kush, and he wrote a poem, for he had been touched by its strangeness and beauty, moved only as one may be moved through an encounter with the beautiful and strange; and he declared he would never be the same again:
(She picks up the guidebook, but does not open it)

Oh the beautiful city of Kabul wears a rugged mountain
skirt,
And the rose is jealous of its lash-like thorns.
The dust of Kabul's blowing soil smarts lightly in my
eyes,

But I love her, for knowledge and love both come from
  her dust.
I sing bright praises to her colorful tulips,
The beauty of her trees makes me blush.
Every street in Kabul fascinates the eye.
In the bazaars, Egypt's caravans pass by.
No one can count the beauteous moons on her rooftops,
And hundreds of lovely suns hide behind her walls.
Her morning laugh is as gay as flowers,
Her dark nights shine like beautiful hair.
Her tuneful nightingales sing with flame in their throats,
Their fiery songs fall like burning leaves.
I sing to the gardens of Kabul;
Even Paradise is jealous of their greenery.

SCENE 2

A hotel room in Kabul, luxurious by Kabuli standards. Two single beds. Milton Ceiling is seated on one bed, Mullah Aftar Ali Durranni is seated on the other. Doctor Qari Shah is standing beside and slightly behind the Mullah; Quango Twistleton is standing behind Milton.
Priscilla Ceiling is seated in a chair behind a bedsheet which has been hung across one corner of the room. There's a lamp on a small table behind her; her shadow is cast on the bedsheet.
A burqa is draped over the arm of a chair.
It's early morning. The mood in the room is very grim.
Doctor Qari Shah is speaking, occasionally consulting a notebook.

DOCTOR QARI SHAH
The conoid tubercle of the left clavicle was found to have been traumatically separated from the conacoid process of the left scapula following severe damage to the conoid ligament, and also the infra spinous fossa quite, ah, shattered by a heavy blow, most probably as the woman was dragged— your wife—by her upper limb, arm that is to say, up and down rubble-strewn streets over piles of bomb debris. After dislocation of the humerus from the glenohumeral joint, there was separation and consequent calamitous exsanguination from the humeral stump. The flexor digitori sublimus and profundus of the middle three phalanges are absent and indicate . . . trauma also, perhaps occurring as the wife attempts self-defense. *(He holds his left hand in front of his face as if warding off a blow)* The, ah, right gynglymus

31

and enarthrodial joints are found to have been twisted to nonanatomical ninety-degree positions and the arm . . . separated by dull force. The right side of the os innominatum is also crushed. Her left leg, the tibia separated by dull force from the femur, snapping cleanly below the lesser trochanter, it may be surmised from the severity of the dermal abrading and bruisings having been caught between two large bits of concrete jetsam and ah, pinched clean off. She is being beaten repeatedly with wooden planks and stakes and rusted iron rebar rods, remember. From the surmisable positions of the assailants and so forth, we believe there were ten persons implicit, approximately so.

My English. I have study medicine in Edinburgh, but long ago. I apologize.

(He pauses. No one moves or says anything. He resumes:)

The axillary fascia of the right, ah, hemispherical eminence, um, mamma, um, *breast*, torn from the axilla, from the sternum, torn off in fact, either by force of a blow or as the corpus is dragged. Her left eye having been enucleated, the left orbit vacant, and canines, molars, incisors absent both her superior and inferior maxillaries, and from dull force many of the skull's two and twenty bones are found to have been compromised, the occiput sheared cleanly off. And consequently to which, spillage of, ah, contents.

It may be ventured there seems to have been no forcible invasion of the introitus. She was not dishonored. Your wife.

(Silence.)

MULLAH AFTAR ALI DURRANNI

She have been torn up. The lady, she, ah . . . Torn *apart*. She have been torn apart to pieces.

MILTON

(Very softly) Oh my God.

32

QUANGO

Bloody, bloody hell.

MULLAH AFTAR ALI DURRANNI

She have wandered through Cheshme Khedre, where undetonated land mines are. She wander alone by the . . . Way ran
nee-hah? *(To Doctor Qari Shah)* How it's said?

DOCTOR QARI SHAH

Ruins.

MULLAH AFTAR ALI DURRANNI

Yes, *ruins* by Cheshme Khedre, where nobody live there any
longer, why she was there? In these bad times, why this lady
your wife come to Kabul? She have been informed upon to
have been not clad in decent attire for street, not wearing
burqa, uncovered. Attack such as this, have never happen
before in Kabul, never in Afghanistan.
Since President Clinton have bombed the people in Khost,
many killed, the people are very angry against Western
aggression-disregard-disrespect for Afghanistan. And also
she have been carrying openly this thing:

*(From a paper sack he removes a yellow discman, headphones
attached, and he hands it to Milton. Milton opens the lid of the
discman, looks at the CD inside, closes it.)*

MULLAH AFTAR ALI DURRANNI

Impious music which is an affront to Islam, to dress like so
and then the music, these are regrettable.

PRISCILLA

(From behind the bedsheet) What is it? May I see?

*(Milton steps behind the bedsheet and hands the discman to
Priscilla. She holds it, then puts on the headphones and pushes*

*the play button. All this is in lamplit silhouette against the bed-
sheet.*
Milton returns, sits on the bed.
*From behind the bedsheet, Priscilla listens to the music and
cries softly.*
The men listen to her cry.)

MILTON

It's, ah, Frank Sinatra. "Come Fly with Me."

MULLAH AFTAR ALI DURRANNI

We search for the criminals who have done this thing, and
when they are seized they shall be put to death. Rough boys,
criminals, and also perhaps they believe incorrectly she is
American.

QUANGO

They've come to claim her body, Minister Durranni.

MULLAH AFTAR ALI DURRANNI

This we cannot know. Where it is.

(Little pause.)

QUANGO

You lost her body?

MULLAH AFTAR ALI DURRANNI

In Cheshme Khedre where these rough boys kill her there is
nearby the UNESCO hospital but this is closed. So she is
taken to the Ladies Hospital though already she is dead. Here
Doctor Qari Shah inspected her remains. For some cause, she
is then transported to Ibn Sena—you say "Avicenna"—
Hospital on Sipah Salar Muhhamad Nadir Kahn Wat. In
Ladies Hospital there are almost no suture, antibiotics, med-
icines of this sort; but as she is dead, this lady, that ought not

to have been considered. Also as well at Abdullah Ibn Sena there is no medicine, anywhere, anywhere in Afghanistan. But this morning hearing you have arrived from Peshawar, coming to call for the dead lady at Ibn Sena, she is found not to be there. Information regrettably is scarce. We are searching now for where she is. You shall stay here. Or return home.

QUANGO
May I ask. With respect. *(In Dari)* Baw tamawmay eh-t'rawm. Chirah bahroyaheen haw zarooree-bood kehgosh baydehand . . . um . . . *(With respect. Why . . . was it necessary for these people to listen to this . . .)* impenetrable litany of medical horrors? To frighten them?

(Ignoring this, the Mullah stands. He turns to Milton.)

MULLAH AFTAR ALI DURRANNI
To you and your daughter, every Afghan heart laments for the mother. Death we know. Kabul is not a city for Western tourist women, we do not want them. In sha' Allah. No thing may be made or unmade unless Allah wills it. He fills our hearts with griefs, to see if we shall be strong. You are kaafer, you do not understand, but this is Allah's way.

(Little pause.)

MILTON
Yes, yes . . . I see. Thank you.

DOCTOR QARI SHAH
I have studied medicine in Edinburgh. I apologize if my English is . . . impenetrable. *(To Milton)* I am truly sorry.

MILTON
No, it's . . . quite good.

MULLAH AFTAR ALI DURRANNI

These also were hers.

(He reaches in the sack and removes three hats, rough wool berets, not like the ones in Scene 1, and a book.)

MULLAH AFTAR ALI DURRANNI

Several fine pacooli. Perhaps gifts for you, her husband.

(The Mullah hands the book to Doctor Qari Shah, who reads the cover:)

DOCTOR QARI SHAH

An Historical Guide to the City of Kabul.

MULLAH AFTAR ALI DURRANNI

But in Kabul now there is no history. There is only God. This is no more a city for . . . *(To Doctor Qari Shah)* Kattel ow tama sha kawol?

DOCTOR QARI SHAH

Sightseeing.

MULLAH AFTAR ALI DURRANNI

Precisely. No.

(Mullah Durranni stands, nods to Milton, who nods back, vaguely; the Mullah leaves the room, followed by Doctor Qari Shah. Quango lingers.
Priscilla pulls the bedsheet down and stays seated, holding the sheet in one hand, the discman in the other.
Milton looks at Quango, speechless.)

QUANGO

You'll want to be left alone now.

PRISCILLA

(Holding out the discman) You'd think a thing like this would be of some value, wouldn't you, on the black market? They'd have nicked it, her assailants, it's what I'd have done if I'd no money.

QUANGO

Music, it's contra Islam, as the Taliban read it. They read it unlike anyone else in the—

PRISCILLA

Yes, and these were very *pious* boys who beat her to death, do you think? All those rusted iron rebar rods, flailing away, and it hasn't a scratch.

MILTON

Japanese plastics, durable stuff.
She's killed herself.

QUANGO

Oh. No, I . . . Shouldn't think so.

(Milton begins to sob.)

QUANGO

(To Priscilla) I should like to help. I shall make inquiries about . . . The body. And I'll . . . call again, if I might, or . . .

*(Priscilla nods, lights a cigarette.
Quango leaves.)*

PRISCILLA

He works for the government? Doesn't seem . . . governmental, what was his name?

MILTON

Twistleton? Bingo? Pongo? Pongo Twistleton? Can that be?
In some semi-official capacity, apparently. There's no embassy,
so . . .

PRISCILLA

Do you think she screamed?
I don't know what she'd sound like if she did.

(They both cry.)

MILTON

She loved you. She did, Priss, she did. We both did. We'll go
home. We'll miss her, dreadfully, but you're young and I'm
not so old and there is the fact of resilience. I shall try to be
for you what she was.

(Little pause.)

PRISCILLA

Yet in this newborn lachrymosity of yours there's nothing
I know of the maternal, which never manifest itself in
mummy in fluid epiphora but rather in fluency, in that sempiternal dyscrasic fluxion of logorrheic blatherskite beneath
the weight of which so much was . . . crushed.

MILTON

(Amused, unnerved) Hah. That's . . . very like her. Sempiternal.
Didn't know you could do . . . that.

(Little pause. Milton points to the discman:)

MILTON

It's all ultimately explained by high-impact polystyrenes.

PRISCILLA

(Tenderly) You've no mystery in your soul, Dad.

MILTON

None. I left that to your mother.

PRISCILLA

What are you going to do now?

MILTON

See it all more clearly, I suppose.

(He starts to cry again.)

PRISCILLA

You're safe in the hotel room, surely.

MILTON

I didn't say I felt unsafe.
Christ I'd kill for a drink.

PRISCILLA

Alcohol is illegal here. And Pongo Twistleton is a character in
a P. G. Wodehouse novel.
I've never seen you cry before.

MILTON

Yes, well, this is what it looks like.
(He takes off one shoe, then cradles it, still crying) I told you
we should never have come! People remain at home when
tragedies happen and the government arranges things like
shipping bodies.

PRISCILLA

The government couldn't even tell us if she was alive.
We still don't *know*.

MILTON

Don't know . . . ?
What?

PRISCILLA

We don't know she's dead.

(Little pause. Milton collects himself.)

MILTON

You're a bright young woman, Priss. You'll rally yourself. We shall respond to this tragedy by growing, growing close . . .

PRISCILLA

(Overlapping) I'm no spaewife, I've no recourse to the extispiscene but I doubt somehow that your confidence in a father-daughter entelechy—

MILTON

Please stop that.

PRISCILLA

Entelechy. It means growth. But people don't grow close from tragedy. They wither is all, Dad, that's all.

MILTON

How did you get so grim? You never used to be so grim, as a little girl you were—

PRISCILLA

It seemed ludicrous to me, all that. "Os innominatum"? What's that, the, the . . . *nameless bone?* What the fuck is *that*? And where's her body then? Something's wrong.

MILTON

What are you—

PRISCILLA

Maybe she's kidnapped. Maybe she's hurt, in a hospital, and they're hiding her for some reason. Maybe she's hiding. From us.

MILTON

Oh that's . . . SHE IS DEAD! *Reuters* has reported it!

PRISCILLA

I'm going out for a bit.

MILTON

Out?

PRISCILLA

Yes.

MILTON

Out . . . SIDE?! You're joking.

PRISCILLA

I'll . . . lose it utterly. I'm going to find her. There are hospitals on this map.

(She picks up the discman, and the guidebook, and starts for the door.)

MILTON

It's *extremely dangerous* out there. Am I to take two bodies home?

PRISCILLA

Better than none.

MILTON

And think, Priscilla, what she must, um, *look* like. You can't want to see that.

PRISCILLA

I don't know. I might.

(She sees the burqa. She picks it up, examining it.)

MILTON

Oh so *here, here* you're choosing to become adventurous? Are
you completely *insane*?
I was being rhetorical. Please don't go.

(She puts the burqa over her head.)

PRISCILLA

(Looking around, through the face-grille:) It's as if I've con-
tracted an exotic ophthalmological condition. A chiasmata.
Or strabismus.
(She removes the burqa)
I mean, Milton, for fucksake, she's my mother, she . . .
Oh God.
(Little pause. Suddenly she screams:)
MUMMY!

(He tries to comfort her. She shakes him off.)

PRISCILLA

Sit here, with you, crying, just waiting, for for nothing, no, can't
do that. You stay here, make calls, call the British Aid man.

MILTON

The bloody telephone probably doesn't work.

PRISCILLA

Of course it—

MILTON

Nothing works here! This is not London! Where's her body?
They ate it, for all we know, this place is that bad it is! And
you may not go out into the—

PRISCILLA

She isn't dead! I know when I'm being lied to. Prevarication/
evasion expert, me. I have been trained.

You ought never to have had kids you two, you really and
truly deserved me.

I'll find her. And if they have ripped her open at least I'll
finally get to see her fucking secrets.

*(She puts on the burqa again and exits.
Milton picks up the phone.)*

MILTON

It works, it . . .
(He jiggles the receiver)
Dead.
(Calling after Priscilla:)
DEAD! DEAD! DEAD!

ACT TWO

SCENE I

On a street in Kabul.
Priscilla is in her burqa, trying to read the guidebook's small map through the burqa's grille, holding it close, changing angles so as to find the strongest light.
A group of women pass by, all shrouded head to toe in burqas, whispering.

PRISCILLA

Um, hullo, can you tell me where the Ladies Hospital is. Or the Red Crescent offices, or the U.N. compound, it's all turned around somehow. Do you speak English?

LADY IN BURQA

(In Dari) Mah nah may donam cheezayk'shomaw may go ayd. Bah cheezabon shomaw harf mayzanayd? *(I do not understand what you are saying. What language are you speaking?)*

PRISCILLA

My mother was . . . They say she was murdered.

LADY IN BURQA

Mother?

(Priscilla tosses off her burqa. She's wearing the discman on a belt around her waist, the headphones in her ears.)

PRISCILLA

Yes! And I am lost. Is this building the—

(The women react with consternation when she throws off her burqa. They hurry off.
Priscilla picks up the guidebook, sits on the curb, lights a cigarette, starts to peruse the map.
Immediately a large bearded man in green shalwah kamiz appears, wearing a black turban, carrying a Kalashnikov and a rubber hose.)

THE MUNKRAT

(In Pashtun) Zan putka! Ow segret-day watchawa! Mukh-kay lahagha cheh woo dey wah hoom! T'yow wah beysharmah khazah yay! T'pah hay zhey cheh dah ayjahzah neshtah. Ghwarla cheh woo wahal shey? Watchawah segret-day! Watchawah bahar, watchawah os! *(Cover yourself and put out that cigarette before I whip you, you shameless idiot! You know that's not allowed, are you asking to be whipped? Put it out, put it out, do it now!)*

(Priscilla, terrified, in a panic, leaps to her feet, dropping the book, throwing the burqa back on, all tangled, the cigarette still in her mouth. She drops the cigarette once inside the burqa and frantically shakes the fabric out, then scrambles to retrieve the guidebook, all the while apologizing.)

PRISCILLA

(Overlapping with the Munkrat) Wait, wait please, I'm sorry, I just . . . keep spilling things and I . . . Wait, wait, stop, I don't speak, I speak English I . . . I am English, British, oh I've dropped my fucking book and . . . Oh fuck I've dropped the lit cigarette, I'll set it on fire, oh my God.

(She throws the burqa off and shakes it out.)

THE MUNKRAT

(Overlapping with above) Sta millah sokh day? Pah kum zai-ikay oseezhee? Dumrah baday woowahum cheh la gar zay dohnah patah shay! Aya t'koom fahishah khazah-yay? Auray cheh zeh sah wayim? Mukh-day putka! T'dayr kassefa khazah-yeh! *(Who is your husband? Where do you live? I am going to beat you till you can't walk, are you some kind of harlot? Can you hear, are you deaf, cover up, you are disgusting!)*

(During the preceding tirade, Khwaja Aziz Mondanabosh enters, watches, then approaches the Munkrat with deference.)

KHWAJA

Meheraboni woklah da gharbi khezah prayzdah. Da zima mass ul yut-day. Z'da hagha maharam-yum. Da injalai zima ur-ra-radah. Da injalai pah charahee Pashtunistan Hotel kay noom-eh sapt k'laydah. Ow hagha-may delta plartahyay rahoowustaydah. *(Please forgive this Western lady. She is my responsibility, I am her mahram, she is my niece, she is a registered guest staying at the Pashtunistan Square Hotel, I am bringing her to her father.)*

THE MUNKRAT

Da khazah wallay yawazay gurzee? Da bil kul yawah fahishah ow lawanda khazah dah. *(Why is she wandering alone then? She's lost, she was exposing herself.)*

KHWAJA

T'khawmakhah munzh dwarlo wobakhah. Da khazah dayr wooraydilay dah ow munzh p'marg-kay sharmay dilay yoo. *(You must forgive us both, sir, she is terror-stricken, and we are both mortally embarrassed.)*

THE MUNKRAT

Ka ko, t'Amreeka yah yeh? *(What, she's American?)*

KHWAJA
Nah, khazah Inglees-sah dah. *(English.)*

THE MUNKRAT
T'pahayzhay cheh zeh bah tahsoh dwarloh woo wah hoom. *(I could beat you both, you know.)*

KHWAJA
Zeh wa'adakawoom cheh dah khazah— *(I will make sure she—)*

THE MUNKRAT
Zeh fekehr kahwoom cheh dah khuzah lezh kootee woo wah hal shee sirf doomrah-cheh haghatah sargandashee . . . *(I think I will, she should be beaten a little, just to make sure she . . .)*
(To Khwaja) T'yahwah khwah tah shah. *(Move aside, you.)*
(To Priscilla, brandishing the rubber hose) Dah day Islami shari'yat mukhaulef kar-day— *(It is forbidden by the laws of the Islamic—)*

(Khwaja steps in between, grabs the hose.)

THE MUNKRAT
T'doomrah joorat kaway cheh z'mah door-r-r-rah neesay khugah! Lass dooray dah khazah tah— *(How dare you grab my whip, you pig! Ten lashes for her and—)*

KHWAJA
(Calm but stern) Dah bah ghalatah kar wee cheh dah khuzah woo wah hal shee. Hagha yawah milmana dah ow dah kho de mil mastiyah deh oosool puhrkhelahv yawah kar-wee— *(It would be wrong to beat her, she is a guest, our guest, it would be offensive to the laws of hospitality to—)*

(Little pause. The Munkrat jerks the hose out of Khwaja's hand.)

THE MUNKRAT

(To Khwaja) Dah khazah bertah hotel tah bozah. Ow zeh nah gharloom cheh tasoh dwarloh b'ya pah sark-kay woo wee noom. *(Take her back to the hotel, don't let me find either of you on the street again today.)*

KHWAJA

Khodaw hafez. *(May God be with you always.)*

(The Munkrat ignores this, and leaves.)

KHWAJA

(To Priscilla, in Esperanto) Ĉu vi parolas Esperanto? *(Do you speak Esperanto?)*

PRISCILLA

What?

KHWAJA

Esperanto?

PRISCILLA

I . . . What?

KHWAJA

That a lady should be unescorted, this is not permissible, but I will be your uncle and show you the city. If by your aimless wanderings and the guidebook I am right in concluding that you wish to see Kabul?

PRISCILLA

Just let me . . . Wait.

(She bends over, breathes deeply.)

KHWAJA

My name is Khwaja Aziz Mondanabosh. You are the distressed lady whose mother was murdered. I am a mahram, the best the city has to offer, I have contemplated upon its every brick, and even better: I am a poet! All Tajiks, we are all poets, but some are not so good, really, they try but I am actually a good poet, quite competent in Dari and even better in Esperanto.

PRISCILLA

Are you Taliban?

KHWAJA

No, Tajik. As I said.

(She doesn't understand.)

KHWAJA

The Taliban prefer Tajiks far away, in Tajikistan. The Taliban are mostly Pushtun and Afghan Tajiks are mostly out of work.

PRISCILLA

You know the city?

KHWAJA

Since 1993 I am a Kabuli. Before that, Earl's Court, ducky. And before that, Kabul, where I was born. Am I to be your uncle or ought I to push off?

(Little pause.)

PRISCILLA

How much would I pay you?

KHWAJA

As you wish.

PRISCILLA

Five pounds for the day.

KHWAJA

As you wish.

PRISCILLA

Is that . . . not enough, or . . . ?

KHWAJA

As you wish.

PRISCILLA

Ten pounds?

KHWAJA

I will be the cheapest family you ever had.

PRISCILLA

How did you know about my mother? That she was . . . ?

KHWAJA

It is a gossipy city, Kabul. Full of widows.

PRISCILLA

Men gossip much more than women. Women give nothing away.
If she was injured, they'd have her in a, a . . . Why can't they find her body? You can't lose a body.

KHWAJA

If she stepped on a mine . . . People are vaporized here. Anything, everything can be lost.

PRISCILLA

But she didn't step on a mine, they said she was torn to pieces. Something about her . . . . occiput. *(She cries)* Her . . . skull. Oh my God.
(She forces herself to stop crying)
Evanition? Or evagation? That is the question.

KHWAJA

I do not know these words.

PRISCILLA

That's why I'm using them. The answer is amphibologous.
I have to stop doing that, it's . . . creepy.
She wasn't brave, you know, she wouldn't court assault, and
she wasn't stupid.

KHWAJA

Missile attacks sour the mood of a city. A pity your mother
did not anticipate Mr. Clinton's intentions.
I shall take you to the hospitals, where sepsis is pervasive.
And to the Minister, who will be unavailable, at prayers,
these ministers are always at prayers. It would be wise to
replace the burqa.

PRISCILLA

I'm . . . You're to be my uncle?

(Little pause. He looks at her.)

KHWAJA

Five years ago in the fighting just three blocks away, a mor-
tar shell and good-bye dear gentle brother, estimable sister-
in-law, nephews, beloved niece.

PRISCILLA

Is that true?

(Khwaja bows a little. Priscilla replaces the burqa.)

KHWAJA

But see, she has returned to heartsick old Khwaja, as all my
dreams foretold.

SCENE 2

Meanwhile, back at the hotel:
Milton and Quango in the hotel room, sitting on the beds.
Quango has a bottle of scotch and they are drinking. Milton
has put on one of the pacoolis.

QUANGO

It's the fifth worst country on earth, according to the Human
Index Rank, not a country, really, a . . . populated disaster.
Thirty-five percent of the kids who survive over the age of
five are drastically malnourished. Most of the arable land is
land-mined.

MILTON

Why on earth are you here?.

QUANGO

I love this place.
This used to be a functioning country, you see? With, ah, sec-
retaries in modest dresses and lady ticket-takers at the cinema. And with cinemas, so they tell me. And standing buildings. Only twenty years ago. It drives a man to drink.

MILTON

I repeat my question.

QUANGO

I answered it, Milton, if I may call you Milton.

MILTON

You may, Mr. Twistleton, if you top me up.

(Quango pours Milton a drink. Milton bolts it.)

MILTON

When I'm alone I can hear her, and smell her; terrible. Her perfume, though I can't recall that she actually wore perfume. If I cease speaking for a moment my limbs grow chilly.

QUANGO

You're in shock.

(Quango pours Milton another drink. Milton drinks it in a gulp.)

MILTON

I've never been so I can't say. I am not myself. I suppose, if you meet a chap in shock, you must allow that you haven't met the chap at all, you've met . . . the shock. Chap's buried beneath, somewhere; shock nullifies the man.

QUANGO

Some hold that shock *exposes* the man. Trauma, grief.
I stay because Afghanistan broke my heart.
I'm an embarrassing sort of person.

MILTON

Nothing embarrassing in admitting that we—

QUANGO

But is it all right to say that, do you think, to say, "It broke my . . ."

MILTON

My daughter broke mine.

QUANGO

She did, did she?

MILTON

Probably actually in the fibers of the cardiac muscles, sorrow causes damage. You shed vitality all along the way.

(Quango pours another drink, Milton drinks it.)

QUANGO

She's quite, quite lovely.

MILTON

She is?

QUANGO

Your daughter.

MILTON

I know who you mean.

QUANGO

Blew my mind.
That's better. Afghanistan blew my mind, Milton. And I cannot get it back.

(Quango pours the last of the bottle, a smidge, into Milton's glass.)

QUANGO

We've drunk the lot.

MILTON

No hope of replenishment?

QUANGO

Not a thimbleful in all Kabul, not that I have access to. It's a notorious crime, drinking, for the commission of which one can jolly well find oneself Toyota-trucked to the old soccer stadium and— *(He makes a gesture of a hand being chopped off)*

MILTON

That isn't true, is it?

(Quango nods yes.)

QUANGO

Many a Friday morning. Leading cause of donor fatigue, or disgust rather; Ban-ban-Taliban. Growing up in a refugee camp, coarsens the sensibilities.
Like a disease, this place.
I've got opium.

MILTON

Opium?

QUANGO

Fancy sharing a bowl?

MILTON

You mean . . . Opium?

QUANGO

Nangarhar Tarballs. Afghanistan's select, haut de grand cru etcetera premiere deluxe.

(Little pause.)

MILTON

Are you a dope fiend, Mr. Twistleton?

QUANGO

Quango.

(Little pause.)

MILTON

My daughter informs me that Quango Twistleton is a character in a novel by . . . someone.

QUANGO

Wodehouse, but that would be *Pongo* Twistleton.

MILTON

And you are *Quango*.

QUANGO

I am actually Dave, but . . . it's a rather stupid story, because my NGO—nongovernmental organization—performs infrequent services for Her Majesty's foreign secretary, we've been deemed *quasi*-NGO by my disdainful purist comrades in the field of human aid. Quasi-NGO, hence . . .

MILTON

Quango.

QUANGO

And since my surname is actually Twistleton, absurd as that may seem, well there you are.

MILTON

Is it a good novel?

QUANGO

Mr. Wodehouse wrote only good novels. Or rather he wrote the same good novel over and over.

MILTON

Are you a dope fiend, Quango?

QUANGO

I'm not, no. Well all right I am a bit of an opium addict. But there's the tradition, you know, Coleridge, De Quincey, Crabbe, Keats, Southey, Shelley, Byron. Oh all right then, heroin. I'm a junkie. Yes. I mean why else would I be here? Afghanistan supplies the world.

I came to do good, biscuits and bandages and woolly blankets. Heroin was a great surprise.

MILTON

So . . . So the embassy in Islamabad, I am trying to comprehend this, has remitted my daughter and myself into the care of a heroin addict.

QUANGO

I hope this will not diminish in your eyes my prospects as a future son-in-law.

That was a—

MILTON

Have you . . . Please tell me the truth. Have you looked for my wife's body? Or don't you actually spend your time away from here—

QUANGO

Shooting up? It's so plentiful here, I need none of the resourcefulness of your typical Western junkie. I afford what I need on my pitiful hire.

I've been to Avicenna Hospital, the Red Crescent HQ on the river, the Ladies Hospital at the College of Medicine or rather what used to be the College of Medicine, the U.N. offices or rather what used to be etcetera, the old Christian Cemetery on Shahabuddin Wat, this morning in fact, to see if there was evidence of recent burial. There wasn't. Your daughter was there. With some old Tajiki cicerone.

MILTON

Was she all right?

QUANGO

Under the burqa, hard to say.

(Little pause.)

MILTON

She refuses to accept that her mother is dead.

QUANGO

Yes, well, for most of us, "Your mum is dead," more or less defines unacceptable.

MILTON

No, I mean she *literally* refuses. She . . .
What is it like, opium?

QUANGO

Nausea at the get-go, then itching, usually, then . . . Peace. Immense dreams.

(He hands a ball of opium and a pipe to Milton, who holds them, staring at them.)

MILTON

How much would it . . . ?

QUANGO

Oh no, I'm not *selling* it, Milton. It's like a toddy. Truly. Helps sleep come.

MILTON

Might not be compatible with my antidepressants. Inadvisable to stop the antidepressants because, well circumstances recommend . . .

I mean she's out to drive me mad, Quango, she's . . . really rather a terrible girl.

QUANGO

She seems . . . Enduring. Without illusion. And of course she is, ah, beautiful, she's really—

MILTON

(Rolling the ball of dope between his fingers) She shouldn't remain here. She's, well, less-than-precisely arranged, she . . . She . . . I suppose I might say this. She attempted suicide. So I am worried. She was eighteen. Some school chum she fell in love with, desperately in love, apparently, she's that kind of girl, he did a runner, and she . . .

She forced me to come. First the one throws away her life and then the other, competing with one another as always, "Me too, me too!" But why must they seek *my* blood?

We had the devil of a time regluing her, and of course you can't, I am forever reminded.

She came home from hospital two years ago and has steadfastly refused to move out, yet in this ghastly place she'll stay out all day.

Revenge. Women are addicted to it.

Opium is a vegetable derivative, is it not?

QUANGO

Bitter milk of the poppy plant.

MILTON

That I should tell such intimacies about my daughter seems . . . *(Shakes his head)* And to a stranger.

QUANGO

A stranger and a dope fiend.

MILTON

And a dope fiend, yes.
You won't share this? That I've told you?

QUANGO

I've got no friends.

MILTON

And yet you seem a bright, agreeable chap.
It relaxes you.
I could do with some relaxation.

QUANGO

As anyone can see.

SCENE 3

Later that day. Priscilla is alone in Khwaja's apartment, very small and poor. She is smoking, reading the guidebook. After a few beats, Khwaja enters, carrying two apples, bottled water and a nan, rolled up.

KHWAJA
I've procured apples and water. I hope you are feeling less queasy. And I have nan, to settle your stomach. And something to tell you. But first I would like to entrust you with something. Here is a sheaf of my poems.

(He holds out a sheaf of pages. She does not take them, she's puzzled.)

PRISCILLA
I detest poetry. Printed matter in general.

KHWAJA
London has such bookshops! Foyle's!

PRISCILLA
They read. She read. I . . . smoke.
(Holding out the guidebook) Take me there.
Cheshme Khedre.

KHWAJA
(Shaking his head no) It is a minefield.

PRISCILLA

It's where they told us she was murdered.
A minefield in the middle of a city. What a godawful place.
What a fucking ghastly place to die.

KHWAJA

As what place is not?

PRISCILLA

We've walked all over Kabul, ruins of this and the wreckage
of that and pillars marking massacres and, and slaughters,
those fucking nightmare . . . *hospitals*. And, and I'm fucking
paying you, so, so where is she? *Where is my mother?*
You see, here in the book. She's marked it. The Grave of Cain.

(Khwaja takes the guidebook and squints closely at the map.)

KHWAJA

No such place exists.
There is here a, a smudge. *(Thrusts the guidebook map toward
her)*
Do you not see what it is?

(She takes the guidebook from him, looks closely.)

PRISCILLA

It's a question mark?

KHWAJA

Yes. This says, not "Grave of Cain," but rather, "Grave of
Cain?" She was pursuing a rumor. On no official map is
there ever a question mark. This would be an entirely novel
approach to cartography. The implications are profound. To
read on a map, instead of "Afghanistan," "Afghanistan?" It
would be more accurate, but—

PRISCILLA

But such an accuracy as might discombobulate more than mere geography and make the hierophants of all fixed order dash madly for cover.

KHWAJA

For someone who doesn't read you have a prodigious vocabulary.

PRISCILLA

It isn't mine.
What are the symptoms of malaria? I feel exhausted. I'm taking nivoquine, it's the state-of-the-art antimalarial, not even the antimalarial-resistant malarial sporozoans can resist. Of course dichlorodiphenyltrichloroethane sprayed over standing water eliminates it, malaria. DDT, it's very toxic, but in this place, who cares about that?
Let's go back out. It's nearly dusk.

KHWAJA

When I was waiting for our nan in the bakery on Flower Street a gentleman—

PRISCILLA

(Again, the guidebook) Take me there.

(Khwaja again holds out the sheaf of poems.)

KHWAJA

Interruption is impolite.

PRISCILLA

They said, when we arrived, don't accept letters, packages.

KHWAJA

They say all sorts of things. Official persons.

These are not for you, who neither speak nor read Esperanto, and who also despises poetry. When you will return to London, might you agree to deliver them? To a fellow Tajik, an Esperantist, Mr. Sahar lives at 17 Pindock Mews, Maida Vale, from Waterloo Station you take the tube to—

PRISCILLA

I know how to get to Maida Vale.

KHWAJA

Politeness shows respect. How to trust someone you do not respect?

PRISCILLA

I don't have to trust you, I'm paying you.
I'm not in top form. You should meet me when I'm not, um, in mourning, furious.

KHWAJA

Are you ever not furious?

(Again he holds out the poems. Again she doesn't take them.)

PRISCILLA

I'd imagine it's hard enough work being a poet in a *real* language. Esperanto poetry seems . . . daft.

KHWAJA

It is a language that has no history, and hence no history of oppression.

PRISCILLA

Sounds bloodless.

KHWAJA

Nothing is bloodless, niece.

When I was twenty-four, I had a good wife and a sweet little girl. I sold vacuum cleaner parts and I was a socialist. A poet must be a thinking man, so I was a socialist, as thinking men often were in those days. But not a communist, no, for what is the world without Allah in it? Fitna, disorder, misery, madness. In 1973 Afghanistan had a go at democracy, and it was the PDPA, the communists, helping Prime Minister Daoud to overthrow Zahir Shah, so I joined them. And Zahir Shah went out, and all the reforms commenced, women literacy campaigns, elimination of the veil, too much too fast. And then there was internal dissent in the PDPA, the military against the intellectuals, and old Daoud was killed, bad, bad 1978. One thing and then another and I was sent to Pole-I-Charki, the prison, and my sweet wife and child went to London, she had family there, the ICRC helped. It had nothing to do with politics, someone wanted the vacuum cleaner shop, my savings.

PRISCILLA

And Esperanto?

KHWAJA

I am getting to that.

I was in prison for six wretched years, during the uprisings, the Soviet invasions, Babrak Karmal was a communist, but when the Soviets put him in he doesn't let me out, why, who can say? It was an appalling time. Dr. Najibullah replaced Babrak Karmal and let some of us out. And that was 1986. He cared for the people, Najibullah. Though he was KHAD, secret police, and he tortured, they say. He was Pashtun, but still not a bad old bastard.

My cellmate in prison had been incarcerated since he was thirty years old, in 1937, so he was when I met him, in 1978, a very old man. He would die in Pole-I-Charki, I would imagine he has died.

I told him I wanted to learn English, I would emigrate to London after I was released, join my family there. He told me he knew something much better than English: an international language, spoken in every country on earth. I had never heard of such a marvel! When my cellmate was young and free, in the cosmopolitan 1920s of old king Amanullah Kahn, Kabulis had been more . . . sophisticated, and my cellmate as a boy had learned Esperanto. Who would not want to be able to speak the world's language? He was a good teacher, a good, patient man, I dream of him from time to time.

He was, unfortunately, mistaken about one important thing. When I arrived in London, speaking only Dari, Pashto and Esperanto, no one could understand me.

I had written three hundred poems in prison, all in Esperanto. I find that I have an ear for its particular staccato music, with its regular system of affixes attached to simple roots, connoting verb, place, opposition . . . I love its modern hyperrational ungainliness. To me it sounds not universally at home, rather homeless, stateless, a global refugee patois.

Sidante en la ĝardeno, mi aŭdis bruon.

Vidante sin en la ĝardeno, mi vokis al si.

Vokite, si tuj venis.

La tera estis tute kovrita de neĝo.

Sidante, atendante, mi aŭdis bruon.

It's nice, no? It was created by a Polish Jew, Zamenhof. He believed that until we could speak to one another in a mother tongue which draws from us our common humanity, peace will never be attained. When I write in Esperanto I am transported to a time when such a thing as a dream of universal peace did not seem immediately crazy. And not even the news that yet another child has trod upon a land mine or has been caught in crossfire can disperse the dovelike murmuring sounds of it. I am moved to compose another lament, in Esperanto, another hymn to peace.

(He holds out the poems again)

17 Pindock Mews.

(Little pause. Priscilla takes them. Khwaja bows.)

KHWAJA
And may the soul of your mother wherever she may be, awake or asleep, witness your generosity.
As I was about to say, before being interrupted: while I was in the bakery on Flower Street, I was approached by an . . . unofficial person. This person knew that you had employed me as your mahram. He has something to tell you.

(Priscilla sits abruptly.)

KHWAJA
Are you well?

PRISCILLA
I'm going to black out. *(She puts her head between her knees)*

KHWAJA
Had I a proper wife, a meal would be available.

PRISCILLA
No, I . . . I'm not hungry.

KHWAJA
That is just as well. For I have no wife.

(She looks up at him.)

PRISCILLA
Please. My mother is . . . not . . . ?

KHWAJA
This man will tell you. He sells hats.
Allah feeds the hungry, He answers prayers.

SCENE 4

In Zai Garshi's hat shop. Priscilla, Khwaja and Zai Garshi.

ZAI GARSHI

Your mother, she wish you to know, she is not dead.
She wish you to know: she have not been killed by anyone,
all this is, ah, invented. She is happy, having met a gentleman. Some heavenly star-spangled night. She have spoken
the kaleema . . .
(To Khwaja, in Dari) Dar zabahnay Inglees-see cheest— *(What
is the English for—)*

KHWAJA

(To Priscilla) The kaleema. It's something equivalent to the
Nicene Creed, but shorter, for Muslims, to say it is to convert.

(Little pause.)

PRISCILLA

My mother is a Muslim?

ZAI GARSHI

Just so! And now she shall marry to a pious Muslim man of
means.
She wish to remain in Kabul, not to see you nor the father of
you, her husband of the past.

PRISCILLA

This is . . . This is nonsense.

WHERE IS SHE?

I'm not fucking stupid you know, I'm SORRY we treated you so wickedly back in, when was it, 1879, but I'm not fucking AMERICAN, *we* didn't fire missiles at wherever it was, YOU NASTY FUCKING PIG, WHERE IS MY MOTHER WHERE IS SHE?

(She hits and slaps Zai Garshi.)

ZAI GARSHI

(To Khwaja in Dari) Aya oh deewan'ast?! Khoh cherah chup nishastee? *(Is she crazy?! And why do you sit here saying nothing?)* OW! *(To Priscilla, in English)* It is truth it is truth I am telling you, stop!

(Khwaja pulls Priscilla from Zai Garshi and holds her till she stops struggling.)

PRISCILLA

Okay, stop, for a moment please.

My mother would never, never . . . do any of this, anything like this. *(To Khwaja)* This man is lying and you're lying and I'm being lied to.

ZAI GARSHI

I am unfinish.

In exchange that this man keep your mother as wife of his, he wish you to help remove now-wife of his who is crazy, first wife, she wish to go away, to London preferably. I arrange meeting of you with crazy first wife. You and this lady leave Afghanistan. Your mother, these have her wish.

(Little pause.)

KHWAJA

The man your mother marries already has a wife, who has gone mad, as many women have in Kabul, the Soviets, the civil wars, the siege, the Taliban, hejab, starving kids, women are so easily driven from their senses. Your mother will live in place of this other woman, who will go to London.

ZAI GARSHI

Precisely.

KHWAJA

This man can no longer live with his wife. Her powerful family agree to emigration, because all want her gone.

ZAI GARSHI

This so-angry woman, as you will see.

KHWAJA

But divorce they oppose.

ZAI GARSHI

She have been a librarian, this lady, Mahala is her name, you will enjoy meeting her.

PRISCILLA

Oh do shut up, my God, shut up. Are you an idiot? Just . . . please.
Why won't my mother see me?

KHWAJA

I cannot answer that.

(Little pause.)

PRISCILLA

I am going to the police.

KHWAJA

That would lead to the arrest not only of this man, and of myself, but also several others who might be killed. The Taliban do not like being lied to, and this is an international embarrassment.

PRISCILLA

GIVE HER BACK! WHERE IS SHE! FUCKING LIAR! SHE'S . . . *DEAD!*

(Pause. Priscilla hears what she's said.)

ZAI GARSHI

(Quietly) If I may speak. *(Pointing to Priscilla's discman, and speaking with reverence)* In the yellow Sony disc player is Frank Sinatra thirteenth album from contract of he with Capitol Records, fateful "Come Fly with Me," yes? Nelson Riddle-Wallah, Axel Stordahl-Wallah, Heinie-Bean-Wallah?

(Priscilla is looking at the discman. She opens it, looks at the CD.)

ZAI GARSHI

You can take my word for it, baby.
Some few of these LPs my parents may they have the perfect happiness of Paradise have leave to me when they are dead, some I have myself to buy at souks in Egypt, Ashkabad, Tashkent, Alma-Ata, airplane tickets to romantic places, yes? But those days and nights like painted kites they went flying by. And after Najibullah and Sibgatullah Mujadeddi and Dostum and Hekmetyar comes the Taliban, yes? They go to extremes with impossible dreams, yes? And so my record player is smashed and all each of the LPs of me, *Popular Frank Sinatra Sings for Moderns* . . . Slips through a door a door marked nevermore that was not there before. It is hard you will find to be narrow of mind.

KHWAJA

He was an actor. The Taliban have closed all theaters, all act-
ing is forbidden, photographs are forbidden, all representa-
tion is sheerk; to make one thing that is like another might
lead one to say that some things are like Allah, and nothing
is like Allah. So the actor sells hats.

ZAI GARSHI

She also have love for Sinatra, your mother, she have with
her pacooli hats and guidebook, marked Grave of Cain,
which she searched in Cheshme Khedre. It is all correct yes?
Now she is appropriate Muslim lady in hejab, she will hear
music never after, as the Taliban insist. She miss this musics
already, your mother. She have great love for musics.

PRISCILLA

She did?
(Little pause)
Tell her . . . Tell her I want to see her.

*(Little pause. Zai Garshi looks at Khwaja, who stares fixedly at
Priscilla.)*

ZAI GARSHI

I will convey.
I was promise that I shall have this LP, ah, *CD*. This is pay-
ment for message as I have convey.

PRISCILLA

She can tell me that herself.

ZAI GARSHI

Yes, please, but . . .

PRISCILLA

Until then, fuck off.

ZAI GARSHI

I would only want to hear. Please.

KHWAJA

It would be an act of kindness.

PRISCILLA

I'm not feeling . . . *Oh for God's sake.*

(She hands Zai Garshi the discman. He looks inside. He closes the lid. He looks up, deeply moved.)

ZAI GARSHI

(Softly) Ah beautiful song that will not die, stardust of yester-day, music of years gone by. Who may solve its mystery? Why shall it make a fool of me? Beg God for peace they say, but something gotta give. 'Round and 'round I go, down and down I go, like leaf in the tide, to this earth of blood and *(In Dari)* tan haw yee. Loneliness. Earthly and unearthly love. Sinatra. A charbetti from Herat, a khandan sung by a woman: guess who sighs these lullabies through nights that never end? Only the lonely know.
(He puts on the headphones)
'Scuse me while I disappear.
(He presses the play button. He listens, eyes closed, and starts to sing "Come Fly with Me":)
> Come fly with me, let's fly, let's fly away,
> If you can use some exotic booze
> There's a bar in far Bombay.
> Come fly with me, let's fly, let's fly away,

PRISCILLA

(Over this, after he's started to sing) And this woman, we're supposed to . . . I don't understand. My mother. Is this the shop in which she purchased the pacoolis, you have seen her. I mean . . . She's . . . well?

ZAI GARSHI
(Continues from above:)
    Come fly with me, let's float down to Peru.
    In llama-land . . .
(In Dari:)
KABUL! KABUL! AAAAH, KABULAY MAQBOOL OH DOST
DASHTANEY YAM, AAAAAH, AAAAH, BAKOOJAW BURDAN-
DAT, AW RAYSO-WAH SHOWKAYTAY TOO MAWRAW MAY
KUSHAD! *(AAAAH, MY KABUL, MY BEAUTIFUL BEAUTI-
FUL KABUL, WHERE HAVE THEY TAKEN YOU, AAAAAH,
AAAAH, MY LONGING FOR YOU IS KILLING ME!)*

*(Khwaja comforts Zai Garshi, then removes the headphones,
pushes the stop button, and hands the discman back to Priscilla.
The two Afghans hold each other.)*

PRISCILLA
What? What did he . . . ?

KHWAJA
(A finger to his lips) Sssshhhhh.

SCENE 5

Priscilla and Milton in the hotel room.

PRISCILLA

Might she have done this? You tell me, she was your wife, is this plausible? I know nothing, me. Daughter of a fucking dictionary of nonsense words, forever apologizing for them, you wouldn't think words nobody knew the meaning of could *be* so *mortifying*, but was she *ever* not mortified? If they *did* beat her to death, she didn't scream, she apologized. Sorry, but I *so envy* you people that you've nothing at all enviable, and sorry for that as well! I always thought her simply selfish and and conceited but I see her now so sickened by the sound of herself and that's not conceit, that smiling humiliated . . . She felt everything she had was stolen, it's why she wouldn't share! Not even the fucking words, wouldn't tell me what they meant, she didn't want me sounding like her, or . . . So of course I'd scamper off to look them up; she filled me full of them that way, withholding: impudicity, glottology, expergisence, glitter and dazzle, beauty and spite. "What's it mean, Mummy, what's it mean?" Me too, huh? Look at me! I'm her! What have I inherited other than her disinheritance?
Ugh. God, I am such a whiny little cunt, a bitter whiny cunt. I'm as dissatisfied and passive as she was. No wonder you hate us so much. No wonder you want us dead.
Well she's not dead, alas alas alas alas alas she is . . . Alive, she's . . .
Why are you listening to all this? Milton? Hello?

MILTON

I've been smoking opium with Quango and it doesn't agree with me.

PRISCILLA

Oh you have not.

MILTON

She is dead.

PRISCILLA

She needs us.

(Little pause.)

MILTON

I've smoked opium. It was pleasant at the time, though it's disagreeable, after. I dreamt of an iron-banded oaken chest full of gold and I fucked it, in my dream. I shan't try opium again, I feel a bit wonky now, I had what felt like a, like a . . . an orgasm deep inside my head, and now I want to go home. Your poor mum. We were incompatible but I did grow to love her. And she's dead, well, it cannot be comprehended. I want to do as she would have me do, Priss, I want to watch over you, to . . . help. I want you to stay, here, with me, and not go roaming, it frightens me too much, the thought of you . . . You are my child. And I want you to, to take a look about you. Think where you are. I beg you, Priss, consider: is this a place in which a crack-up is advisable?

PRISCILLA

I'm not cracking up. You *thanked* that man, that Mullah Whatsisname. "Thank you," you said. You're scared is all.

MILTON

And you have a past record of mental affliction.

PRISCILLA

I don't. I'm not crazy. I attempted suicide. Lots of people
attempt—

MILTON

Lots of people are crazy, Priscilla, that proves—

PRISCILLA

I don't have to fucking *prove* anything, Milton, I was *upset.*
I was eighteen years old, so I, so I swallowed pills and . . . oh
why am I bothering to—
Be a *little* brave, Dad.

MILTON

No, but I'm not brave and I've never been and know what?
I've no wish to be. You see? None. Never have. Let go. What?
Do you think she—what? In secret collusion with these men,
that Mullah, that doctor, with Reuters for Christsake, she
invented that horrible death so that . . . simply so that she
could vanish? It's mad. And, and, she . . . *married* a Muslim?
Which, allow me to point out, she might just as easily have
done in London, and a nice Western sort of Muslim too, not
one of these . . . barbarians. So that she can spend the rest of
her life in what must never have been more than a
Himalayan bywater at the best of times, draped in parachute
sheeting stirring cracked wheat and cardamom over a
propane fire? And why concoct this hoodoo of disassem-
blage? They might simply have said she was shot, or stepped
where she oughtn't to have stepped, or for that matter she
could have called and said, "Hullo, I have met a desperately
gorgeous Afghan chappie and I have become his umpteenth
wife and sod you lot, you will see me no more a-punting
down the Thames." These people who are the ruthless crea-
tures of a culture, if I may call it that, a culture of betrayal
and brutality and dissembling, are practising on you, they
see you as . . . vulnerable. If I weren't here with you I've no

doubt you'd fall for the whole jabberwocky and would be arriving at our flat tomorrow with some Afghan lady whose name is composed entirely of gutturals and sounds like a toilet backing up, "Here's Mrs. Wargarwazbaz Bizooli Waza, Dad," then you'd help her unpack her—what is it? *Burqa?*

PRISCILLA

Go fuck an oak chest, Milton.

When I took those sleeping pills I was pregnant.

(Little pause)

She moved all this, didn't she, out of the house, out from under all that crying in the kitchen nights when nobody could hear and into the great world beyond where people who hate . . . *murder* one another, we're far beyond fathers and daughters and all that, *you* look, look what she's done, where she's brought us. We're at the stage of blood sacrifices, right? And and I take her point. Spot on, Mummy!

MILTON

I didn't know that.

PRISCILLA

Killed the, the fetus.

Good we're not Catholic. Is it a sin, if the killing's oops unintentional? Oops. Dead. Oops. She could have been Catholic. Calvary was always before her, suffering for those she saw suffer. Useless.

MILTON

I didn't know you were going to have a baby.

PRISCILLA

Not a lot you did know, Milton. She knew. I told her and told her. She just . . . couldn't talk about it. All those words, but not a one for me.

(She goes to him. She hugs him. He stands there, not responding.)

PRISCILLA

She isn't dead.

(Milton gently pushes Priscilla away. He goes to his bed and lies down, curled away from her.)

PRISCILLA

She's fled us. She isn't dead.

SCENE 6

The next morning. Mahala is in a rather elegant room, seated on a chintz-upholstered sofa. Priscilla, Khwaja and Zai Garshi stand.
Mahala speaks continuously. rage and urgency; she barely waits for the translation, if at all.

MAHALA

Where are the women of Afghanistan? Can you tell me this? Ces gens parlent Pashto, ces etrangers, ces occupants, ces Talibani; Kabul speak Dari. Vous le saviez? Ce sont des nettoyeurs ethniques. *(These people speak Pashto, these strangers, these occupiers, these Taliban; Kabul speaks Dari. Did you know this? They are ethnic cleansers.)*

KHWAJA

(Translating haltingly, a few words behind Mahala, starting after "parlent Pashto") These people speak Pashto, these um . . . strangers, these occupiers, these Taliban. They are . . . ah . . . *(In French, to Mahala)* Nettoyeurs ethniques?

MAHALA

They seek to . . . destroy all who are not Pashtun.
(In Dari) Een haw khod raw Mullaw maygoyand, manzooram Ulamaw ast, een haw khod raw dar shawlay payombar paychawneeda, refugee camp gutter rats az Jalalabad wa Qandahar may auyand, walay een haw bah ferosh-ay taryok wa mawod-day mukhaderah, wa ba kushtar-ray atfal

maypardawzand, wa ba dushmanawnay-shawn reshwah may dehand taw bahonhaw zameenah-ay moowahfaqeeyat raw barroyay on haw muyahsar sozand. *(They call themselves mullahs, the ulema, they wrap themselves in the Prophet's mantle, these refugee-camp gutter rats from Jalalabad, from Khandahar, but they sell drugs and murder children and bribe their enemies to give them their victories.)*

KHWAJA

(Translating, overlapping) They call themselves mullahs, the ulema, they wrap themselves in the Prophet's mantle, they are from the camps, and from Jalalabad, from Khandahar, they sell drugs and murder children and bribe their enemies to give them their victories.

MAHALA

Atrocities they commit. People are flayed alive. The skin remove, yes? Yes! Bake to death lock in metal trucks in the desert. Thrown down . . . Des sources. Wells. And where is America?

PRISCILLA

I . . . I'm from the—

MAHALA

(Continuous from above) The CIA posylaiet denezhnyie sredstva etim ubliudkam cherez Pakistan, gdie vooruzhionnyie vlasti, c'est tout les Pashtuni-wallah, sumasshedshikh i terroristov, auf die eine odere andere Art werden sie an den Tueren alle ihrer Herren erscheinen, but still Se She Ah platit im den'gi, posylaiet im oruzhiie. *(The CIA sends these bastards funding through Pakistan, where the military high command, it's all Pashtuni-wallahs, these madmen and terrorists, they'll turn on their masters sooner or later, and still the U.S. pays them money and sends them guns.)*

ZAI GARSHI

This lady says CIA pay the Taliban through Pakistan. I personally do not—

MAHALA

America buys this, bombs, from Communist Chinese to sell in secret to Taliban through Pakistan. Afghanistan kill the Soviet Union for you, we win the "Cold War" for you, for us is not so cold, huh?

PRISCILLA

I'm not—

MAHALA

(Almost continuous from above) The gas pipe of Unocal! For U.S., yes? Il faut subir le Taliban so all must be calm here so gas . . . *flows* to ships, for American profit, to . . . to . . . Afin de vaincre L'Iran! Pour que les États-Unis puissent régler un compte de vingt ans avec L'Iran! *(So that Iran can be bested! We must suffer under the Taliban so that the U.S. can settle a twenty-year-old score with Iran!)*

KHWAJA

(Translating, starting after "Afin de vaincre") We must suffer under the Taliban so that the U.S. might settle a twenty-year-old score with Iran.

MAHALA

(Not waiting for Khwaja to finish) You love the Taliban so much, bring them to New York! Well, don't worry, they're coming to New York! Americans!

PRISCILLA

I'm English.

MAHALA

English, America, no difference, one big and one small, same country, America say, Britain do, women die, dark-skin babies die, land mine, Stinger *projectile*, British American so what? So what you say?!

Trente mille veuves habitent la ville, trois cent milles enfants à nourrir, et le travail leur est défendu! À la bibliothèque on donnait aux mendiantes du pain et du thé, qui-est-ce-qui leurs en donne maintenant? *(Thirty thousand widows live in the city with three hundred thousand children to feed, and they're not allowed jobs! At the library we would hand beggar women bread and tea, who gives them bread and tea now?)*

KHWAJA

(Translating, after "à nourrir") There are three hundred thousand widows and children who may not work. At the library they gave away tea and bread. She worries now that . . .

MAHALA

(Not waiting for Khwaja) They have close library! Library! This is Islam? Muslims are les gens du Livre. Scholars! Poets! Les peintres, les compositeurs, les philosophes, les mathématiciens, nous savions comment marchait l'univers des siècles avant vous, nous avons inventé l'énumeration et le zéro et la médecine! Et ils ont fermé la bibliothèque! *(The people of the Book. Painters, composers, philosophers, mathematicians, we knew how the universe worked centuries before you did, we invented counting and the zero and medicine. And they've closed down the library!)*

KHWAJA

(Translating, after "avant vous") And Muslims have been through history educated people. We were once in advance of the West in knowledge. So the Taliban have closed down the—

MAHALA

Le Quran ne suffit pas! *(The Quran is not enough!)*

(Khwaja indicates to Mahala that he won't translate that.)

MAHALA

The Quran these cannot read! Illiterates and child murder-
ers. Nettoyeurs ethniques. Suray char, seporahyay noh
(Arabic: surah four, chapter nine): "Let people fear the day
when they leave small children behind them unprovided."
(In Dari, to Khwaja and Zai Garshi) Wah too khodraw mard
may donee? Shomaw ranj may barayd? Maw ham bayshtar
ranj may baraym? Shomaw een hawlat raw bar-r-r mardom
nayah'wardayd? Shomay jon yon wa washeeyon wa shomaw
atfal-ay ton raw az gurusnaygee nah maykushayd? Shomaw
een raw eejawzah nah maydehayd? Kee eenraw eejawzah
maydayhad? Ayah shomaw fekehr maykonayd een Islamast?
*(And you call yourselves men? You suffer? We suffer more. You
permit this? These criminals and savages to enslave and
oppress your women? To make your children starve? You
allow this? Who would allow this? You think this is Islam?)*

PRISCILLA

(To Khwaja) You stopped translating.

KHWAJA

She is railing at us. She calls us effeminate men.

MAHALA

Not "effeminate," this I do not say. I say women are braver
than you men of Kabul. Queen Gawharshad rule half the
world from Herat. Malalai insist to you: kill the British
invaders, she insist and so then you do, because she, *she* have
the courage. Young girls have march and die to fight communist and the Russian soldiers, but you, you do not die, you do
not march, nothing from you while we starve in rooms,
because these "heroes," they make you feel like not pious
Muslim, because you want a coward order, *le fascisme.* I go
mad, British, I cannot cease shouting all day, a bird, a bird

taps the window, I shout at these bird, *"Die, break your neck at the glass!"* I am so bitter of . . . of . . . De L'Âme? L'esprit?

PRISCILLA

Spirit? Soul?

MAHALA

I pray to God let all birds of the air be curses to fall on Kabul with dead eyes and broken necks. Je suis bibliothècaire! Je veux me promener encore une fois. Je veux aller en soirée encore une fois. Je n'ai rien à lire! *(I am a librarian! I want to walk down the streets again. I want to go to parties again. I have nothing to read!)*

Des femmes, elles se meurent tout autour de moi, je les entends mourir dans leurs maisons quand je regarde furtivement par la fenêtre, quand je me promène dans ma burqa. Ma cousine, sa fille, elle s'est pendue. Ma vieille amie Ziala Daizangi, Hazarra de Bamiyan, s'est jetée du toit de— *(Women are dying all around me, I can hear the sounds from the houses when I peek out the window, when I walk in the burqa. My cousin, her daughter, she has hanged herself. My old friend Ziala Daizangi, Hazarra from Bamiyan, threw herself from the roof of—)*

KHWAJA

(Translating, after "soirée encore une fois") She wants to . . . *(After "je n'ai rien à lire")* She is a librarian. She wants to go out and to parties. She has no books to read. *(After "fenêtre")* She hears women die, sounds of this come to her from, from . . . *(After "Bamiyan")* Her cousin hanged herself and—

MAHALA

Ziala Daizangi, she I have known thirty forty years? Hazarra family from Bamiyan, the family of she now in Qetta, refugee camps. This one dies, that one starve, that one exploded, shot, rape, rape, die, die, die, die, die, whole family, whole

family of she, all Daizangis of she, husband of she, children,
she throw herself off roof! Taliban not to permit burial and
I cannot go to see the body of my friend, my family afraid, no
mahram will come and her body, what did he do? Her uncle?
There are dogs in the street? Ziala body have been left in the
street for dogs? In my dreams, always, she does not come to
me, her body is in the street, as it fell. I miss . . . I miss . . .
(She weeps)

(Little pause.)

ZAI GARSHI
Usually she is cheerier.

PRISCILLA
Do you want to go to London?
Your husband . . . has married my mother. Is this true?

(Mahala weeps, hides her face, and rocks.)

PRISCILLA
You've actually . . . seen my mother? Alive? Today?

*(Mahala crawls on all fours to Priscilla, grabs her hand, kisses
it. Priscilla, horrified, tries to pull her hand away. Mahala will
not let go, holding onto Priscilla's fingers.)*

PRISCILLA
Please, please don't.

MAHALA
To leave is a terrible thing. But I must be saved. Yesterday
I could not remember the alphabet. I must be saved by you.

(Priscilla pulls her fingers from Mahala's grasp.)

Act Three

SCENE 1

Priscilla and Khwaja in an alley near Mahala's home.

PRISCILLA
That poor woman. My God.

KHWAJA
Simply one of millions, many many millions who—

PRISCILLA
Yes but I've not *met* them, I've *met* her.
When she . . . crawled and grabbed my hand and kissed it
I thought oh fuck she'll have the fingers right off my hand . . .
She wouldn't let go. As if she was drowning.
You . . . *watching me*, you think I should take her. To London.

KHWAJA
I said nothing of the—

PRISCILLA
And that bit about birds, she's . . .

KHWAJA
Perhaps she is going mad.

PRISCILLA

She isn't mad, she's fucking furious. It isn't at all the same. What was her name? I didn't get her . . .

KHWAJA

Mahala. You overlook or fail to hear things.

PRISCILLA

I do?

KHWAJA

A great many things, niece. Like most of the young you choose to contemplate rather than to observe. This is why the Prophet commands us to travel when we study. Go to China, He told us, to learn about Allah. Talib, it means "student," did you know? And also "traveler."

PRISCILLA

I'd think . . . I dunno, observing the world is what disillusions you, when you're young, then you turn inside.

KHWAJA

The worst disillusion stems from how impossible it is to know one's own unsociable soul.
(Little pause. He removes another packet of poems from his bag)
Perhaps, even if you refuse to save Mahala, you would be willing to take with you another packet of poems to—

PRISCILLA

Oh, Jesus, would you *stop*? You, first, first you ask me to take this stranger to London and . . .

KHWAJA

(Softly, under her) It is not I who have asked you to . . .

PRISCILLA

(Continuous from above, right over Khwaja) . . . and then, and then, oh here, these poems, and what next, packets of white powder? I can't help you, her, half the days I can't roust myself out of bed.

Tell her, I mean tell this man to tell my mother, no tell her yourself: if she is alive she will see me and . . .

(She stops, hearing herself)

Oh. She's dead. What am I . . . ?

Tell her I have to see her, her in the flesh, or you can all die for all I care.

(Little pause. He shakes his head no.)

KHWAJA

She has asked Mr. Garshi to say to you that though she is not dead, you must think of her as dead; for she has relinquished everything of that life which you know to live in another world.

(Little pause.)

PRISCILLA

She could write something, then. Or, or she could see me, this is cruel. *(She's crying)* I mean, no, I don't believe she's . . . She's dead, that's all, you're . . .

KHWAJA

She will not write. She says she is an Afghan now and shall not write or speak until her hands become hands that write Dari and Holy Arabic, until she can recite the Suras by heart and his kisses have changed her mouth she will neither write nor speak, not to you, especially not you. You are a danger. She loves you too much. Don't hold her back from traveling.

PRISCILLA

You mustn't embroider. Or I'll think you a liar.

KHWAJA

I am a poet, it is not possible that I lie.

She has told him to tell you this: you have suffered and will suffer more yet, she fears, because your heart which is a loving heart is also pierced through. She prays now to Allah who forgives all who sincerely repent, to forgive her and through her penitential loneliness, to forgive her daughter as well.

(Priscilla is crying.)

KHWAJA

Mahala's passage papers through the tribal areas, her exit visa across the Khyber Pass to Pakistan, these have been prepared. A sponsorship letter would bring her into the British embassy in Islamabad. English chap, Mr. Twistleton, he has such a letter.

PRISCILLA

She bruised my hand. Look. My fingers are stiff. It's . . . like a curse.

SCENE 2

Milton and Quango in the hotel room. Quango holds a square of tinfoil, which contains a small lump of white powder—heroin—over a cigarette lighter. Milton, guided by Quango, sucks the smoke rising from the heated powder through a straw. Once Milton inhales, Quango indicates that he should draw the smoke deep into his lungs and not exhale. Milton does, and is flying immediately.

QUANGO

Off you go, Milton. Star of your own movie, you are, flying carpet over minarets in the moonlight.

(As Milton is enjoying his rush, Quango turns to the junkie's apparatus he's laid out for himself. As he speaks he lights a candle in a holder, then shakes powder from a packet into a spoon, carefully.)

QUANGO

They say the Taliban all have purloined videocassette players. The buggers are particularly fond of *Titanic*, you know, "Leo, Leo . . ." . . . Sentimentality being a predictable concomitant to ferocity and indomitability. Theirs is a landlocked country, but if anyone should be able to understand the metaphor of a ship foundering, it's the Afghans.
(Holding the spoon over the candle)
Heroin stanches sentiment. I thought it so simple when I first arrived, Man A wants X, and why Man B denies him, and

I shall help them both. 'Tisn't . . . simple, you'd have to be God, look down on Afghanistan, high up hallucinatory cinematoscope: turn it turn it, night and day I do that: no way out for the Afghans. Pakistan over there, supporting the Taliban, give them Afghanistan as a distraction from their *real* dreams, and . . .

Have you noticed their remarkable jade-colored eyes?

MILTON

We live near Pakistanis in London, Ghulupa or Palavi, when they're out for a walk it's husband first, wife next, then the kiddies, like a little train of crocodiles.

QUANGO

How are you feeling?

MILTON

Oh, it's lovely, heroin is much superior to opium!
What are *Real* Dreams?

QUANGO

What? Oh, the *Big* Dream: Pashtunistan. The Pashtuns of Afghanistan and their near-relatives, the Pathans of Pakistan dream of creating it by joining Afghanistan with Pakistan's North-West Frontier territory. Major worry for Pakistan, that.

MILTON

I am still very sad about the missus.

QUANGO

Well of course one would be, it's only been three days—

MILTON

For she is dead, my deranged daughter's desperate delusions notwithstanding. But heroin heals the heart.

(Quango ties a cord around his upper arm, palpates the vein, shoots up.)

MILTON

Ouch.

QUANGO

No, it's . . . Yin and yang. After the yin pinch, puncture, there's . . . mmmm . . . Lovely.

MILTON

It is lovely.

QUANGO

Not as lovely now as it was in the beginning.

MILTON

Like marriage.

QUANGO

I am unmarried.

MILTON

Or like children.

QUANGO

And fantastically lonely.

MILTON

No lovely or at least cooperative girls about?

QUANGO

None. Well, whores, but sad, shabby whores, the real girls all locked away, shrouded like . . . like . . .

MILTON

Like shrubbery against the frost!

Do you realize . . . I actually said the word "fuck," meaning copulation, right in front of my own daughter. Is it the drugs, or do you think I might still be in shock?

QUANGO

Or maybe you're just a rubbishy old git.

(They laugh.)

MILTON

If I am it is you who have made me, Traitor-Angel! Spirited Sly Snake! So get thee gone!

QUANGO

Where shall I go?

MILTON

Pashtunistan!

QUANGO

Can't do, it doesn't exist.

MILTON

Let us establish it!

QUANGO

Pakistan would not approve.

MILTON

Well fuck Pakistan, then! Been wanting to say that for *years*! Nice juicy bite out of Pakistan, would it be? Pashtunistan? And Pakistan is not large.

QUANGO

No.

MILTON

India is large.

QUANGO

Yes.

MILTON

India is . . . *enormous*.

QUANGO

Yes it is. So the Pakistanis keep the Taliban with Afghanistan and plans for Pashtunistan lay by. But the longing for it poisons the region: the Taliban export their desperation. Turn it turn it. This way it's Pakistan, that way Shi'ite Iran, and the Sunni Taliban slaughtering the Shi'ite Hazarras, pleasing Sunni Pakistan and Sunni Saudi Arabia and their overlord the sunny United States which has smiled down on the Taliban until—

MILTON

Until last week when America bombed them! *(He laughs)* It's down the rabbit hole!

QUANGO

Killed quite a number of people actually. Ten, twenty-eight, forty-eight, a hundred and eight, depending on the source.

MILTON

Osama bin Laden!

QUANGO

No, they missed him.

MILTON

Opium farmers, then!

QUANGO

Not in the desert, Milton. You're, uh, spoiling my high.
Have you noticed, nearly every other man you meet here is
missing pieces?

MILTON

(Proud of this) I've not left this room since we arrived!

QUANGO

Reagan was right about them, they are . . . the bravest people
on earth. Fucking gorgeous.

MILTON

I thought you said heroin didn't make one sentimental.

QUANGO

I'm in love with your daughter.
I am.

MILTON

Naaaaaaah you're not, you want to roger her, but be warned:
she is fertile and then she bombs the innocent inhabitants of
her womb with sleeping pills, because, as I said, she is not at
all *lovely*. Leave the dead in their graves! But she will disin-
ter. She's a born digger, she was born with a spade in her
hands. The little ghoul. Prowling the streets for her mother's
cadaver to drag home in her teeth, needing to *see* it, I suppose, *see* the underside of her own mother's ribcage. She'll
leave nothing in peace, no sore unprodded, no injury forgiven
and nothing *ever* heals on the jackal bitch's scabby hide. *(He
starts to cry)* My wife has died, horribly died, and I shall be
alone with her when we are home and she with me, and I am
all she has left, and we are neither of us what anyone wants.
Jesus Christ on the cross, she was my daughter, and you
know, you know, I don't care much for kids but I really love
babies, I love babies, and she has killed my grandchild, my
progeny, she was a pink pearly little marvel once but she has

betrayed me, she chooses NOW! NOW! Can you imagine?! To tell me this! Her own father! That she aborted! As if we'd nothing between us, as if I'd . . . no *interest*, as if . . . Cunt is right! Cunt is right! And I have turned into this . . . man who sees his daughter, smells his mad lost daughter festering in her room and wishes *evil, evil things to befall her* . . . Ah Christ.
(He shudders)
I must lie down. Queasy all of a sudden.
(He does)
Don't think I'll discuss family affairs no more, me, I'm . . . *Really* dizzy.
(He begins to drift off)
Sing me a song of Pashtunistan, far, far away . . .

QUANGO

There is no song to sing.

MILTON

Frank Sinatra, then. *(Sings sadly:)*
   Way down among Brazilians
   Coffee beans grow by the billions . . .
(Faint chuckle) Awwww, *brilliant*, that . . . *(Sings again:)*
   You date a girl and find out later . . .
   Dah-dahdah dah, something . . .
   Her perfume was cooked right on the grill . . .
(Nodding out) Have they coffee crops in Pashtunistan? Anything to export, labor for . . . pentium processor chip assemblage, or . . . ?

QUANGO

Poppies. An oil pipeline . . .

MILTON

Something like that, golden, golden . . .

QUANGO

From Khazakstan and Uzbekistan, from Turkmenistan through Afghanistan, oil flowing to Pakistan, and never through Iran, nor Moscow nor New Delhi, golden energy from the Caucasus to the sea, to Western free democracy, past ghostly Pashtunistan alive only in the heart's plans of every Taliban man and each Pathan . . .

(He sees Milton has gone to sleep)

Ah, Milton? You do not care for the geopolitical? Lord Emsworth was looking through the wrong end of a telescope at a cow. "It was a fine cow, but like most cows it lacked sustained dramatic interest." Wodehouse. Apex of Western Civilization.

(He opens Priscilla's suitcase)

I suppose I could sniff her knickers, or put on her bra or something.

Have a wank.

(He buries his head in the suitcase, roots around. He finds a bottle of pills. He holds them up and gives them a shake)

Antimalarial? Antidepressant? Abortifacient?

(To the unconscious Milton:)

Give my regards to the damsel with the dulcimer. Don't drown in your own saliva.

(He removes a pair of Priscilla's panties. He sniffs them, then puts them on his head. Slips a hand in his pants and tries to get hard, have a wank. He puts his panty-covered head in her suitcase, still trying to beat off. The door opens and Priscilla enters in her burqa, quietly. She takes in the scene: Milton unconscious on his bed, Quango with his head in her suitcase, doing something nasty.)

PRISCILLA

(To Quango) What the fuck are you doing?

(Quango sits bolt upright, falls backward. She pulls off her burqa. He yanks the panties off his head, stumbles over to gather up his shooting works. She shoves her clothes back in her suitcase. As this is going on:)

PRISCILLA

Oh God, you . . . You were in my . . . You . . . Jesus. What the fuck were you two . . . Jesus.

QUANGO

I'm . . . *(He giggles, mortified)* Blame it on the drugs, please, I do such stupid things when I'm stupid and—

PRISCILLA

GET OUT!

(Quango turns to leave.)

PRISCILLA

You have a, a . . .

(Quango stops.)

PRISCILLA

I've been told you have some official letter? If I wanted to get someone from here to London, you have a—

QUANGO

You're not serious. For, for the, the Afghan lady who . . . ? Your dad says he won't agree to—

PRISCILLA

Oh, so he told you. About . . .

QUANGO

Yeah.

PRISCILLA

Chatterbox, him.

QUANGO

He is that.

PRISCILLA

His opinion is . . . They said she knows people in London.

QUANGO

They always say that.
In Islamabad they'll run checks and, you know, to certify she's not a terrorist. And you're, ah, unemployed, that'll make it harder to—

PRISCILLA

She's a librarian, she's not a terrorist, and should she turn out to be a terrorist well I could give a fuck.
How do you know that? That I'm unemployed?
What else did he tell you?

QUANGO

Um, only that your mum is . . . that you *think* she's . . .

(Milton suddenly snorts, starts, and, still asleep, lurches to his feet. Priscilla and Quango watch him. He looks about, not see-ing. He picks up Priscilla's suitcase, as if going on a trip. He walks to the bed, lies down, and falls fast asleep again.)

QUANGO

I was helping him relax.

PRISCILLA

You succeeded
(Gesturing toward her suitcase) You relaxing too?
He's shattered. You'd no right to . . . It's wrong.
You do not inspire confidence, "Quango."

QUANGO

Dave.

PRISCILLA

"Quango."

QUANGO

Do you really think your mum would actually, you know. Was she, your mum, was she—

PRISCILLA

I don't want to talk about her, all right?
Least of all to you.

QUANGO

To be sure, I just . . . Yeah. It's an intro letter to the Peshawar people who then have to pass you up to the Islamabad people at the embassy. Getting an Afghan woman through the—

PRISCILLA

But you have the first step.

QUANGO

Of a steep staircase at the top of which is London. And who would not want to ascend?
I'll trade it you.

PRISCILLA

Trade it.

QUANGO

You might not give a fuck but should she turn out to *be* a terrorist, it'd be *my* name on her permissory letter, do considerable damage to the trajectory of my, ah, career, that would. But for a toss? A tumble? For the—

PRISCILLA

You're joking.
What on earth makes you think I'd . . . ? Are you out of your—

QUANGO

Yes. Yes. Definitely yes. Bit too long in the sun. Desperate? In love? Desperate in love? Yep. It's me. You seem like the best

shot in forever, not a, a lady journalist or a, you're, well I figure it's unlikely but fire away, that's the motto of the
Twistletons, that is, just—

Just give me the fucking letter, Dave.

Fuck you I shan't. Sorry. I mean, sorry about it all, your . . .
horrible da and, your mum, who by the way is *dead*, I mean,
I don't mean to be vicious but everyone dies here, fatal place
really, sort of house special, death is. Here's a good one, stop
me if you've heard this, bloke named Aurel Stein? Expert on
Buddhism, spends sheer *decades* trying to get into Afghanistan and when they finally give him an entry permit, after
forty fifty sixty years of applying (you see letters of passage
here are not of small consequence) *finally*, aged eighty he
gets in, his octogenarian heart's desire, Afghanistan! Goes to
Kabul, drinks water: typhus, dysentery, malaria, diarrhea,
ready-for-it rimshot—death! Another bone-load for the Christian cemetery. And she's dead too. She must've intended it, a
woman? Flying to Kabul in 1998 for a bit of sightseeing, a
lark? Face it for fucksake, she *topped herself. I'm sorry but she
bloody did.* Guess the proclivity for oblivion runs in the family.

What's that mean?

Oblivion? Proclivity?

He told you?

Or, or rather she got some poor Afghan street sods to do her
topping for her, and—

PRISCILLA

He told you. About my . . . And what else?

QUANGO

But if, but if you've no more love of yourself and your bloody easy life than that, if you don't care to be alive at all, why scruple at anything? If you're just throwing yourself away, couldn't you have sex with me first? Am I worse than dying?

PRISCILLA

(Overlapping) He told you, all that, he, he . . . and and you think it turned him on, *offering* you me, or was it just to punish me for . . . Or maybe he knew you'd spill the beans, just as you've done, and, you know, then I'd learn how precious a thing I am to him, be sure I'll move out when we . . .

QUANGO

(Overlapping) Stop, Please. I . . . I should never have said any of . . . I'm, it's inexplicable, the . . . It sort of made me feel like, I don't know, protective, hearing you'd tried to hurt yourself, I felt . . . angry, I dunno, I—

PRISCILLA

And what else? What else did he—

QUANGO

The abortion. That.

(Pause.
She stares at him. He looks everywhere else.)

PRISCILLA

(Quiet, confused, sad) But he . . . All that?
But I'm his daughter. And he doesn't even *know* you.

(Another pause. Then she goes up to him and kisses him, a deep long kiss. He stands frozen still while she does it.)

QUANGO

Please. Stop. I'm . . . sorry.

PRISCILLA

You're a junkie, right? Needles? Are you clean? Well never mind, I wouldn't believe you, have you got condoms?

QUANGO

I . . . Yes.

PRISCILLA

One condom.

QUANGO

Yes.

PRISCILLA

God you're really desperate. I'm . . . worse.

(She puts the burqa back on and heads for the door. She stops and turns back to him.)

PRISCILLA

Well?

QUANGO

Nights like this I know I'll never get clean. More than likely die in Kabul.
You've made me so lonely, Priscilla.

(Little pause. She starts to say something, then stops.)

PRISCILLA

I guess you lead the way.

(He goes out, she follows.)

SCENE 3

So late at night it's nearly dawn, but the sky is still black and wild with fierce stars.

An open place, mountains of rubble. Terrible fighting took place here.

A Marabout, a thin old Sufi hermit, sits by a small fire which he stirs from time to time with a stick. He is reading a book.

There are signs posted warning of the danger of undetonated mines.

Near him there's a depression in the ground, a rectangle of cleared earth outlined in small white stones, about five feet long and a foot and a half wide. A flame in a pot burns at one end.

Khwaja enters leading Priscilla, who is in the burqa, holding the guidebook.

KHWAJA
Step carefully! It's terribly dangerous here!

THE MARABOUT
(In Arabic) Heqoul alghaam. *(Land mines.)*

PRISCILLA
What did he . . . ?

KHWAJA
Land mines.

THE MARABOUT

(In Arabic) La budda an takoona magnoonan letaseer hona mortadian burqa'a. Qoul-laha an takhla'a haza al burqa'a. Barak Allah-hu feek wa ya'ahteeka al salaam. *(Only a fool would walk here in a burqa. Tell her to take it off. May God bless you and grant you peace.)*

KHWAJA

He recommends that you remove the burqa.

PRISCILLA

Is it safe?

KHWAJA

Safe? No, it's a minefield, it's past curfew, it's nearly dawn and the Taliban patrol the area. It is everything safe is not. Why have you brought me here?

(Priscilla takes off the burqa.)

PRISCILLA

I'd trouble sleeping.
We're leaving. In just a few hours.
I wanted to see this place.
(To the Marabout) This is Cheshme Khedre?

THE MARABOUT

(In Arabic) Na'am, Cheshme Khedre. *(Yes. Cheshme Khedre.)*

PRISCILLA

(To Khwaja) Who is he?

THE MARABOUT

(In Arabic) Ana marabout fee haza al-makaan. *(I am a marabout in this place.)*

TONY KUSHNER

PRISCILLA

Is that Pashtun or Dari?

KHWAJA

Arabic. He is a marabout.

PRISCILLA

A marabout is . . . a Sufi hermit.
It's in the guidebook. You see, I have learnt things.

KHWAJA

Travel is good for that.

THE MARABOUT

(In Arabic) Enanni a'eeshoo fee zalek al hotam. *(I live in the rubble there.)*

KHWAJA

He says he lives here.

PRISCILLA

(Looking about for a house) Where?

KHWAJA

In the rubble.

PRISCILLA

He lives in the . . . ?

THE MARABOUT

(In Arabic) Laqud ta-a'a-hadtoo an abqa hona toual al sanawaat al baqeeyah fee hayatee. Aqoomu betanzeef al maqbarah almuqaddasah, wa abqee al sho-a'a-lah muqadah, wa osa-a'e-d al hogaag a'al al salah. *(I have taken a vow to remain here for all the years left to my life. I keep the Holy Gravesite clean, I keep the flame going, I help pilgrims pray.)*

KHWAJA

(In Arabic) Fahemt . . . *(Pointing to the depression in the ground)* hona? *(I see. It's . . . here?)*

(The Marabout nods yes.)

KHWAJA

(In Arabic) Meen madfoon hona? *(Who is buried here?)*

THE MARABOUT

(In Arabic) Owwalu owlaadu Adam. *(Adam's first son.)*

KHWAJA

Remarkable. Every day, something new.

PRISCILLA

What?

KHWAJA

It seems we have found what you sought. This is a grave.

PRISCILLA

Whose?

KHWAJA

According to the gentleman, Adam's first son.

PRISCILLA

Oh.
(She stares at the grave)
I thought I'd, I dunno, there'd be some sort of sign . . . for me here. That she'd marked the map for me.
Please ask him, this man, if he was here when she was attacked.

(Khwaja pauses; then:)

KHWAJA
(In Arabic) Imam. Laqod qarraroo anna ommaha qod qootelet hona, ow kareeban min hona. *(Imam. Her mother was reportedly killed here, or near here.)*

(The Marabout shrugs.)

KHWAJA
(In Arabic) Innaha kaanat ta'amel, ala ma-a'a-taqed, an tageeda now-a'an min . . . *(She was hoping, I suppose, to find some sort of . . .)*

THE MARABOUT
(Confused, bemused; in Arabic) Hal kaanat tazoonu anneha sategat ommahaaa hona? Fee allayl? Fee Cheshme Khedre? *(Did she think she would find her mother here? At night? In Cheshme Khedre?)*

KHWAJA
(In Arabic) Robamma. Innaha— *(Perhaps. She is very—)*

PRISCILLA
Last night I dreamt if I came to this place I'd find her. She'll meet me here.

(The Marabout looks up suddenly, apparently seeing someone. He points in the direction in which he's staring.)

THE MARABOUT
(In accented but good English) Ah, and here she is!

(Priscilla and Khwaja turn in the direction the Marabout's pointing.
They stare, watching, waiting. They wait and wait for a long time. No one comes.
The Marabout watches this for a moment, then goes back to his book.)

Khwaja gives up first. He turns back to the Marabout, then back to Priscilla. She keeps staring, waiting.
No one comes.
Khwaja touches her shoulder. She turns away. She looks at the Marabout, who pays her no attention.)

PRISCILLA

Why did you . . . ?
(To Khwaja) Why did he say that? Did he see someone?

(She turns back to look again.)

THE MARABOUT

(Pointing to the grave; in Arabic) Hal targhab fee asalah fee al maqbarah al-moqadash? *(Would she like to pray at the Holy Gravesite?)*

KHWAJA

He wants to know if you would like to pray at the gravesite.

PRISCILLA

Oh. No. I mean . . .
Why did he say he'd seen my . . . ?

(Priscilla looks one more time in the direction the Marabout's indicated.
Khwaja sits on the ground near the grave.)

KHWAJA

He was marked. Everywhere he tried to rest, people drove him away. Only Kabul, they say, did not. This has always been a hospitable city.
But it was a great mistake, burying him here. They should have driven him away.

PRISCILLA

(After a beat, still looking off) How do you know he was welcomed? Does anyone die peacefully in Kabul? Perhaps he's buried in Kabul because he was murdered here.

KHWAJA

It might explain things. God had warned us: hands off. That's why Cain was marked.

PRISCILLA

(Returning back to Khwaja) I thought it was to reveal his guilt, his shame.

KHWAJA

No. He was marked as a warning: hands off. He who murders the murderer would be punished sevenfold.
(Looking about at the ruins) Even if he was murdered: sevenfold, a thousandfold, all this seems to me . . . excessive.

PRISCILLA

It's the worst place on earth.
(Looking at the grave) It's probably an empty pit.

KHWAJA

(Shrugs) Every grave is empty, every grave holds nothing but dust.

PRISCILLA

Anybody could be buried there.
(She sits by the grave, opposite Khwaja) I don't have the letter. Couldn't get it.
I'm sorry I forced you here. We've brought our misery to your city, my family. I'm sorry. For the trouble.

KHWAJA

(Nods his head yes; then suddenly, fiercely) What have you ever brought us besides misery? Gharbi? Ferengi? The West? And many among us would like to give your misery back to you.
(He shrugs, exhausted)
You have to take home with you nothing but the spectacle of our suffering. Make of it what you will.

PRISCILLA

I, I lied, I have the letter.
She's my mother, I can't leave her here. I'll keep looking, if she isn't dead she'll *want to see me*. Eventually, she will.

KHWAJA

And Mahala?

(She takes the letter out of her pocket. Holds it out to Khwaja. He doesn't take it.)

PRISCILLA

I can't save her, no one will save her. She'll just . . . die. She's just one of the pople who dies, and no one minds, she's a . . . a *corpus vile*. That's a body, alive or dead, of no regard to anyone. *(The letter)* I don't want this. I don't want to do this.

KHWAJA

Corpus vile. So many odd words.

PRISCILLA

My mother's.
(She looks at the Marabout) How do I pray?

(The Marabout unrolls a small, ancient, threadbare prayer rug, places it near the grave. He indicates that Priscilla should come to the rug. As she approaches it, he holds out an old clay cup.

He rattles it: a few coins inside jingle. Priscilla finds a coin in her pocket, drops it in his cup.)

PRISCILLA

I'm not Muslim, this is so stupid.
(She kneels on the rug)
May I tell you something? She won't come.
A junkshop, her, discarded needs, pamphlets from defunct societies for dashed hopes, loss, loss. All her forgotten words: Cosmolatry. Idolatrous worship of the world. Cosmognosis, that's a lovely one, the secret knowledge an animal has, a bird for example, which teaches them when to migrate and where to go. *Corpus vile.* She was a mother who demanded interpretation. She loved everything the world's forgotten. It's why she came here.
And we'll leave her here. In Afghanistan. So at the heart of the world the world's forgotten it.
(Little pause)
I should go to the hotel. Tell Mahala. We'll leave half eight, a taxi to the Khyber Pass. He won't be happy, but. I'll try to take her to London.

KHWAJA

Your mother will be so pleased.

PRISCILLA

My mother is dead.

(The light is changing, night giving way to dawn. A muezzin's call for prayers.
The Marabout stands.)

KHWAJA

He wants to go now. To the mosque for dawn praying. I too.

PRISCILLA

Yes.

(She kisses the earth of the grave)
Poor Cain.

(She stands.
The Marabout rolls up the rug, tucks it under his arm.)

THE MARABOUT
(To Priscilla, in Arabic) Hafazakee Allahu ala al-dawaam.
(May God keep you in His embrace forever.)

KHWAJA
May God keep you in His embrace forever.

(The Marabout leaves.
Priscilla hands Khwaja the discman.)

PRISCILLA
Please give this to Mr. Garshi. His recompense.
(She takes a twenty pound note from her pocket)
And for you.

(Khwaja receives it, bows. He produces another sheaf of papers.)

KHWAJA
One last packet of poems for Mr. Sahar.

(Priscilla takes the poems.)

PRISCILLA
17 Pindock Mews.

KHWAJA
My little poem, the one I recited? You never asked what it meant.

PRISCILLA
What did it mean?

KHWAJA

It is very simple. It is about someone waiting in a garden, in the snow.

Deep within, someone waits for us in the garden. She is an angel, perhaps she is Allah. She is our soul. Or she is our death. Her voice is ravishing; and it is fatal to us. We may seek her, or spend our lives in flight from her. But always she is waiting in the garden, speaking in a tongue which we were born speaking and spend of what we love to learn.

Go home with care.

SCENE 4

Milton and Mahala are sitting in a desolate concrete room. There is perhaps a barred window with mountain peaks visible outside, or perhaps they are visible outside the door. A Taliban Guard is also present, also sitting. He has a Kalashnikov and ammo belts. There are a few boxes of papers, and on the walls, lists of government edicts and quotations from the Quran in Arabic.

MILTON

The electromagnetic spectrum—including the visible rainbow as well: color is a perceived property of frequency, thus-and-so-many pedahertz . . . Or is it terahertz? Well, ten to the fifteenth or ten to the eighteenth, it's . . . Let's see. It's hard to explain.

MAHALA

We say: "We have taken the coloring of God, for what better hue is there?"

MILTON

Do you, now?

So, all right then, imagine a number of people in a darkened room and each has a torch, or, or a lantern, many different lanterns, each with a different colored flame. And let us say that it is my task to sort them all, to, to banish confusion, to send him here, send her there, through this or that door. This is what I do. Now how do I do this?

In my work, we have things which we call "duals," pairs of two things which are alike but also opposite. Frequency is one thing, um, *capacity*, in a sense, it occupies the dimension of space. And time is another, the opposite of space—and yet in computer network engineering, these two opposites may be looked at as a dual, a, a single thing, in that information, language, may be sent along either the long axis of time, one thing following another, or along the short axes of frequency and amplitude, height and width.

(She smiles and nods, trying to follow him.)

MILTON

It's, well, without the maths, it's . . . It's like shouting down a pipe, what I do, how loudly must you yell, what language must you yell in, what other languages and yelling chaps have their mouths wrapped 'round this pipe, who's on the receiving end, though, orthogonal to what we are discussing, well, that's more software and I am hardware, I . . . very seriously doubt that I am making myself understood.

MAHALA

I do not understand.

MILTON

No I'd think you wouldn't. I'm often told that I'm more than ordinarily inept at explaining science to laypersons. It's an unforgiving place, science. If you don't speak its language it spits you out peremptorily.

MAHALA

It is I who have failed. My English.

MILTON

It's . . . very good.

MAHALA
Years of not speaking . . . .

THE GUARD
(In Pashtun) T'bayaday ekhpul chahdaree pah sar klay. *(You should put on your burqa.)*

MAHALA
(In Pashtun, fierce hiss) Moolsah! T'dah chardare pah sar kah! Kalakhar! *(Drop dead! Put on your own burqa, you shit head!)*

(Little pause.)

MILTON
What did he say?

MAHALA
He ask if I shall like a glass of water. I tell him I did not. He is so polite boy.

THE GUARD
(In Pashtun) Tamawmay mardhawyay Inglees koonee-astand. Ekhpul mah shookatah dah woowayah. *(All British men are homosexuals. Tell your boyfriend that.)*

MAHALA
(Overlapping, in Dari) Birow-woo dohborah saray kish'zorat day konay Pakistanee. *(Go back to the farm, Pakistani peasant.)*

(Little pause.)

MILTON
I'm sorry you know, it's not that I don't want you to come to London.
My daughter isn't well and she'd no business offering.
(Little pause)
She believes my wife has married your husband.

MAHALA

I am told this, yes.

MILTON

My wife is dead. She was killed.

MAHALA

I am not told this. I am told she, my husband, marry. I am told.
I . . . am needing to come to London.

MILTON

Pakistan might have to do. You have papers to get through
the border, but. London.

MAHALA

Refugee camps in Peshawar. No one, no one care to see that
this one, that one has dead. Death.
(She shakes her head no)
Parlez vous français? Deutsch?

MILTON

English is my only language, alas.

MAHALA

English, and, ah, *science*. "Hardware." "Duals."

MILTON

Oh! Yes.

(Mullah Aftar Ali Durranni enters. Milton and the Guard stand.)

MULLAH AFTAR ALI DURRANNI

(To Mahala, in Pashtun) Munzh-tah parwah neshtah cheh
chertazeh. Angleezee injalai seh asnod cheh deh Afghanistan
day Islami Imawrat marboo tadah warsara dah. Ow haghah
dah waw kawee cheh asnodo deh haghah la boxna relah

shawneedah cheh woorsarah oos neshtah. *(It doesn't matter to us if you leave or where you go. The English girl has papers belonging to the Islamic Republic of Afghanistan. She claims they were stolen from her luggage. They are not with her.)*

(Pause.)

MULLAH AFTAR ALI DURRANNI
(In Pashtun, with menace) T'khawmakhaw bayad mawtah za wab raw klay! *(You must answer me!)*

MAHALA
(In Dari) Agar man bakhshawyesh az shomaw jenawbay Mullah saheb. May khaw ham shomaw bawyad khaw he sheh maw raw qabool conayd. *(If I ask for mercy, Minister Mullah Sahib, you must grant it to me.)*

THE GUARD
(In Pashtun) Mullah saheb, haghah khazah droghjana-dah. *(Minister Mullah Sahib, she is a liar.)*

MILTON
Might someone tell me what's going on?

MULLAH AFTAR ALI DURRANNI
Have you remove or witness to be remove from chest . . . *suitcase* of your daughter a, a paper? Many paper?

MILTON
Visas? We gave them to the man who asked for them when we arrived here. Mr. Twistleton in Kabul, on behalf of the British government, he authorized the—

(Mullah Durranni holds up his hand for silence, and Milton stops talking.)

MULLAH AFTAR ALI DURRANNI

Other paper.

MILTON

For . . . You mean for her? But you see, we aren't responsible for—

MULLAH AFTAR ALI DURRANNI

(Again the hand) Other paper. Not visa. Strange language paper.

MILTON

I don't know what you're talking about. May I see my daughter, please? I would like to see her now.

MULLAH AFTAR ALI DURRANNI

Soon, please, sit.

MILTON

No, not soon, this has gone on long enough, for two hours we've been sitting here, now please bring her here to me or bring me to her or—

(Mullah Durranni sweeps out of the room, and as he leaves he nods to the Guard who ratchets some ratchet on his Kalashnikov. Milton sits. The Guard sits.
Pause.)

MILTON

(To Mahala) Do you think she's all right?

MAHALA

I think we shall be very quiet.

MILTON

Do you know what papers he's talking about? What are "strange language papers"?

(Little pause)
In a sense, strange languages is what networking is about.
Languages expressed as binary code, numerical sequences,
ones and zeroes, digitally reducing the unmediated slovenly
complexities which exist, let us say, analogically in space, by
making of complicated nuanced things their simple non-
nuanced identicals, which exist not in space but in space-
frozen-and-rendered-sequential, in time, one nothing one
nothing nothing one, you see. I'm afraid I rattle on when I'm,
well, afraid.

MAHALA

One nothing one nothing nothing one. Sequences of codes of
numbers, as with for example the Dewey Decimal System!

(He looks at her with considerable surprise.)

MILTON

In a sense, yes.

MAHALA

(Making the connection) By which knowledge is to change to
les fiches de reference, to numerals, which . . . metaphor,
represent.

MILTON

Yes, yes, just so! But how improbable! How do you come to
know of the Dewey Decimal System?

MAHALA

International for libraries.

MILTON

You're a librarian?

MAHALA

I have been being for vingt, ah twenty year, librarian.

MILTON

Ah, yes? "Où est la bibliothèque?"

MAHALA

Ah bon, très bon, mais j'avais l'impression que vous ne parliez pas français? *(Oh good, very good, but I thought you didn't speak French?)*

MILTON

No, no, it's the sum total of my first form French, "Où est la bibliothèque," I've no idea why I said it, um—*urge* to communicate, I suppose. In our dire straits. I'm . . . Hah! Quite a good deal less frightened than I'd have thought I'd be. Kabul has emboldened me.

MAHALA

Bold, yes. Kabul. Lion.

MILTON

I am worried about my daughter, I would like her to reappear, though I am also quite cross with her, she's disobeyed her father. Your daughters, I'd guess they don't do that, disobey?

MAHALA

My daughters, all Afghan daughters, are slaves now. Beaten killed.

MILTON

Yes.

Thoughtless of me, I'm . . . sorry about all that.

MAHALA

(A flash of anger) Tosh. You care nothing all that, Afghan daughter.

(Leaning in, an odd small smile) Listen, British Sahib, it is . . . *OK. My problem.*

MILTON

No, that isn't true. I . . .
Yes, well.

(Little pause.)

MAHALA

Mr. Dewey, great . . . prophet, philosophe, progress, America progress? Reason, the mind, l'Utopienne.

MILTON

Ah, that was *John* Dewey, um . . . Pragmatic philosopher, one of those chaps, wrote something about religion and reason being not opposed, adversarial, but, ah, conjoined, intermarried.

MAHALA

Alike, opposite. A "dual."

MILTON

Yes. Good!

MAHALA

Join together to . . . banish confusion!

MILTON

Banish confusion, that's networking, yes! Excellent! Joining opposites, routing, like . . . married couples crossing a threshold.

MAHALA

Networking, routing, threshold.

MILTON

Energies, urgencies traverse a passing-through place, an . . . intersection.

MAHALA

Intersection. Like Afghanistan.

MILTON

I don't . . . Oh. Yes. *Precisely! Precisely!* Right under our noses, the perfect metaphor! Afghanistan! Armies, and, and gas pipelines, licit and illicit markets, and even Islam, communism, tribes, the incommensurable interests of the West and the East, heroin, missiles, refugees, and each is a language, moving chaotically.

MAHALA

And you shall . . . make machine making to banish confusion?

MILTON

Well, for starters, this will interest you, my company voluntarily participates in a libraries computerization scheme, you know, we are putting the entire catalog online.

MAHALA

What means online?

MILTON

Oh. Anyone who has a, who can buy one, a computer, can, with the touch of a button, peruse the entirety of the British library collections catalog, millions of books I should think, if not billions.

MAHALA

Millions of books? Not possible.

MILTON

Oh yes. Without leaving home. Day or night, everything ever written, there at your dining table with the flick of a—

(Milton sees that Mahala is crying.)

MILTON

Oh, I'm sorry. Why are you . . . ?

MAHALA

Poor Afghanistan.

(Priscilla enters, wearing a headscarf, carrying the burqa, looking haggard.)

MILTON

Are you all right?

MAHALA

(To Milton) Please take me to London.

MILTON

Priscilla?

(Priscilla shakes her head and shrugs, indicating: "I don't know.")

MILTON

You haven't been harmed?

PRISCILLA

(Indicating Mahala) This isn't about her Milton. They don't care about—

MILTON

Are we going to be released? Can we call ahead to—

PRISCILLA

(To Mahala) It's about the fucking poems.
Did you—

(The Mullah comes back in. The Guard stands again.)

MULLAH AFTAR ALI DURRANNI

(To Priscilla) We shall want again to search the suitcases.

PRISCILLA

I would give you the bloody things if I knew where they were. Why do you *want* them?

MILTON

(Overlapping with Priscilla) What poems?

PRISCILLA

They're in *Esperanto,* for fucksake, they're of no use to anyone!

MILTON

(Overlapping) What are you talking about? Esperanto poetry? Why do you have Esp—

PRISCILLA

They were given me.

MULLAH AFTAR ALI DURRANNI

Gift?

PRISCILLA

Is there an export tax on . . . Yes. Gifts.

MULLAH AFTAR ALI DURRANNI

To . . . to read?

PRISCILLA

I guess so.

MULLAH AFTAR ALI DURRANNI

Do you know this . . . Espre . . . What shall you call it?

PRISCILLA

It's . . . What difference does it—

(The Mullah raises his hand.)

PRISCILLA
Esperanto. Oh God this is so stupid.

MULLAH AFTAR ALI DURRANNI
You speak this . . . Esperanto?

PRISCILLA
(Simultaneously with Milton) I do, yeah.

MILTON
(Simultaneously with Priscilla) Of course not. No one does.

MULLAH AFTAR ALI DURRANNI
(To Priscilla) Speak it please.

(Priscilla is silent.)

MILTON
No one speaks it, not anymore. I would really like to know what this is about.

MULLAH AFTAR ALI DURRANNI
Your daughter have with her paper with informations. She have been seen with spy.
(Sternly) You have hire this Tajik mahram. He is said to have give you papers. Written in language so no person can read, these papers you are to give to person in London. These papers are not of poems but Tajik informations for Rabbani and Massoud. Placements of weapons and this. Written in . . .
(To Mahala, in Pashtun) Shefer? *(Code?)*

(Mahala doesn't look at him.)

MULLAH AFTAR ALI DURRANNI
Code. How it's said.

They have tell you this woman is wife of Muslim man, Kabuli man who have marry dead British woman, she have not die. *(To Milton)* Yes?

MILTON
It's . . . Do you know where my wife's body is? Why has it not been found?

MULLAH AFTAR ALI DURRANNI
This woman is Pashtun woman, crazy woman, who she is? She is doctor wife, Doctor Qari Shah. *(To Mahala)* This is not so?

(Mahala looks at Priscilla, then looks down.)

MULLAH AFTAR ALI DURRANNI
You think Doctor Qari Shah marry your wife? You think he make story, whole story? Just for you? *(Indicating Mahala)* She have flee him, he may demand with witness she shall be killed. Useless woman. USELESS WOMAN!

(He nods to the Guard. The Guard ratchets the Kalashnikov again. Mahala screams.)

MULLAH AFTAR ALI DURRANNI
(To Mahala, in Pashtun) Senadoona roklah. Zeh pohayzhoom cheh tah saradah. Kah raw naklay, woo bad day wazhnoom. *(Give me the papers. I know you have them. Give them to me or I will have you killed.)*

(He advances on her, screaming at her; she slouches out of the chair onto the floor, covering herself with her burqa, sobbing.)

MULLAH AFTAR ALI DURRANNI
(In Pashtun) Maw tah raw klah os! Maw tah raw klah os! OS! OS! OS! *(Give them to me now! Give them to me now! NOW! NOW! NOW!)*

PRISCILLA
(Overlapping) Oh my fucking God, he's—

(She runs at the Mullah. The Guard shoves her to the ground.)

PRISCILLA
He's going to kill her, MILTON, STOP HIM!

MILTON
I have over two thousand pounds. Please do not kill her. I will give you all the money I have. Let us go. We don't have your papers. My daughter knows nothing of any of this, this is your problem entirely, not ours. Here. *(He takes out his wallet and proffers it) Here.* Take. Please do not shoot this woman.

(Mullah Durranni stares at the wallet, then at Milton, for a rather long time. No one moves.)

MILTON
I . . . I am asking you, sir, to please allow us to take her with us, and to leave. We really don't know where . . . Please.

MULLAH AFTAR ALI DURRANNI
You ask me to take bakhsheesh. Wog take bakhsheesh, yes? This is crime in Afghanistan. You shall put this away.

MILTON
You, you take bribes. I've been told, you people take bribes. This is a bribe. I've been told you're not so pure. This is a bribe. Take it, please. I don't mean to insult you, sir, but you can't shoot her.

MULLAH AFTAR ALI DURRANNI
You want her?

MILTON
I don't want to watch her die.

MULLAH AFTAR ALI DURRANNI
We shall shoot her in other room.

MILTON
Please. Take.

(Little pause. The Mullah takes the wallet, throws it on the floor at Milton's feet.)

MULLAH AFTAR ALI DURRANNI
(Wearily, calmly) Afghanistan is Taliban and we shall save it. No one else shall, no one else care. England betray us. United States betray us, bomb us, starve us to . . . *distract* on adulterous debauch Clinton and his young whore. *This* is good for woman? Islam knows what dignity a woman shall have. U.S. and Russia destroy us as destroy Vietnam, Palestine, Chechnya, Bosnia. As India destroy Kashmir. As Tajikistan and Uzbekistan and Kazakhstan keep Islam from its people. As U.N. deny Taliban to be recognize. All plot against Islam. Iran plot against Islam. For five thousand years, no one shall save Afghan people. No one else but Allah may save it. We are servants of Allah.
(To Mahala, in Pashtun) T'dah shayroonah lahray. Zeh baday loos koom, ow b'ya baday pah goolay woo wah hoom. *(You have these poems. I will have you stripped and then shot.)*

(Mahala shakes her head no. She holds up her empty hands. Pause. Mullah Durranni looks at her.)

MULLAH AFTAR ALI DURRANNI
(Tired, giving up; to the Guard, in Pashtun) Zah larlashah ow deh haghah boxoona pah motor-keh watchawah. *(Go put their suitcases on the truck.)*

THE GUARD
(In Pashtun, pointing to Mahala) Dah bayad talashee shee? Munzh b'ya dah khazah deh dah talashee deh parah woogooroo,

loy Mullah saheb. *(Shouldn't she be searched? We can get a woman to search her, Minister Mullah Sahib.)*

MULLAH AFTAR ALI DURRANNI
(In Pashtun) Zah bastanayoh pah lahree-kee watchawah. Haghah sarah asnoh doh nishtah. *(Put the suitcases on the truck. She doesn't have the papers.)*

THE GUARD
(In Pashtun) Khadah, magar-r-r— *(Yes, but—)*

MULLAH AFTAR ALI DURRANNI
(In Pashtun) Zeh cheh seh wayoom, haghah watchayah! *(Do as I tell you to do!)*

(The Guard exits.)

MULLAH AFTAR ALI DURRANNI
Doctor Qari Shah does not demand death of her, she is of nothing to any Afghan man. She shall die in sewer of Qetta or Peshawar, she shall not be for London. British embassy shall certainly refuse entry. You have lie to her.
Truth is truth. We seek what has been revealed to the Umma, what is higher and more complete. May Allah forgive you and may you find your way to submit to Allah.
(Smiling but serious) If not, go to hell.

(The Mullah begins to leave.)

PRISCILLA
What . . . Please, what has happened to Khwaja Aziz Mondanabosh?

MULLAH AFTAR ALI DURRANNI
I know no such man.

PRISCILLA

To my mahram? To the Tajik mahram who wrote the . . .

MULLAH AFTAR ALI DURRANNI

Tajik mahram have been arrested and executed. For treason against the Islamic Emirate of Afghanistan.

PERIPLUM

London. 1999.
In the same room as Act One. Mahala is dressed like a modern
English woman. She looks very different. She has been reading.
Priscilla is standing in an overcoat.

MAHALA

It has been a long while.
My English has meantime improved.

PRISCILLA

Are you sleeping with him now?

MAHALA

Your manner meantime has not improved.
It has been difficult for me. But it is lovely here.
(The book in her hands) I am reading the Quran again. For
all those terrible years, I was too angry. I am myself becom-
ing Muslim again. The Book is so beautiful, even in English.
In Arabic its beauty is inexpressible.

(Little pause.)

PRISCILLA

He wanted to shoot you. The mullah.

MAHALA

No. He did not. He is not so bloody as that. We, our families,
Durranni Pashtun, and he and my husband had been

comrades-in-arms. Mujahideen group Tariki-I-Talibani. I am no farmer's wife, little Bibi Nobody. Since I was a girl, I . . . *intimidate* everyone, and this perhaps has saved my life.

PRISCILLA

I saved your . . .
Forget it.

MAHALA

Your newfound reticence becomes you.

PRISCILLA

Did he shoot Mr. Mondanabosh?

MAHALA

This I can't know, but it is likely, I fear.

(Pause. Priscilla starts to cry, then stops herself.)

PRISCILLA

I'm not going to ask you about my mother.

(Silence.)

MAHALA

I am lying, you think. I loathe the Taliban, they are my own people but I loathe them. You think I have lied to help bring from Afghanistan the poetry of Mr. Mondanabosh, which are not hymns of peace in dream language of universal brother-hood but military information for the Northern Alliance.

PRISCILLA

Who sound as dreadful, really, as the Taliban.

MAHALA

We hope not so. Better for women, not as God-crazy. Not agents of Pakistan. On the other hand, Massoud, Rabbani

are Tajiks, not Pashtun, so will the Afghans follow them? Or will Afghanistan without the Taliban sink again into unending civil war, with missiles supplied by the West?
In Afghanistan, Priscilla, the choices are frequently narrow.

(Little pause.
Priscilla sits.)

PRISCILLA
I've got a job. Proofreading computing manuals. Dead-boring work. Tell him, it'll horrify him.

MAHALA
He regrets. He feels in Kabul he—

PRISCILLA
He thinks I'm innumerate. I'm trying to forgive him, it's hard. Almost as hard as forgiving her.
(Little pause)
I can't imagine her. Wearing the clothes she'd be wearing, the food, the hunger, trying to speak—that's the hardest, her not knowing the words . . .
Did she leave because she had to leave? Did she leave because of love? Did she die, or flee, or . . . ? I never could understand her. Not her words, not her distance, not even her grief. "What's it mean, Mummy, what's it mean?"

MAHALA
Perhaps, in going to Kabul, she gave you an answer.

PRISCILLA
I don't know if she's alive or dead.

MAHALA
Vous m'avez sauvée, Priscilla. You have saved me.
She gave you . . . responsibility. For a life.

It could be that she has embraced a new being. A suffering woman of Afghanistan. Though she chooses what no Afghan woman would choose.

PRISCILLA

No. We're people of terrible luxuries.
Sometimes I think they're what Afghanistan needs, the Taliban. Anything anything for certainty. I get the appeal of fascism now. Uncertainty kills.

MAHALA

As does certainty.
They're like the communists, the Taliban. One idea for the whole world. The Dewey Decimal System is the only such system.

PRISCILLA

It provides no remedy.

MAHALA

Only it provides knowing, and nothing more.
(Little pause)
I am gardening now! To a Kabuli woman, how shall I express what these English gardens mean?
Your mother is a strange lady; to neglect a garden. A garden shows us what may await us in Paradise.

PRISCILLA

She read instead.

MAHALA

I have examined her library. Such strange books.
I spend many hours. The rains are so abundant.
In the garden outside, I have planted all my dead.

(As the lights fade, in the garden outside, a nightingale.)

END OF PLAY

AN AFTERWORD

When the Twin Towers collapsed I was standing on a rainy beach on the Dingle Peninsula in Ireland, watching my four-year-old niece and her newfound playmate, a little British girl, splashing about in a tidal pool. I noticed a crowd gathering around a nearby car radio; I joined it just as the second tower came down. Minutes later, the beach was abandoned. Everyone went home to wait for what seemed like the end of the world.

The next day, as my sister and I tried to get back to New York (it took five days), I received emails from a few newspapers asking for an article about the attack. I imagine everyone who'd ever written anything was asked to write about the attack. I refused. I've never been shy about offering opinions, but opining felt hasty, unseemly and unwise. One of the papers was gathering short essay responses to the question: "What is the meaning of 9/11?" This on 9/12. I thought about the wisdom of Jewish laws of *shiva*, the weeklong period of silence, retirement, prayer mandated as one begins mourning. I didn't write.

A month later, as the cast of *Homebody/Kabul* was beginning rehearsals at New York Theatre Workshop and letters containing anthrax spores were arriving in newsrooms all over the city, I was asked to prepare a statement for the press, since it was assumed that, given the subject of the play, there might be controversy. This is what I wrote:

> *Homebody/Kabul* is a play about Afghanistan and the West's historic and contemporary relationship to that country. It is also a play about travel, about

knowledge and learning through seeking out strangeness, about trying to escape the unhappiness of one's
life through an encounter with Otherness, about
narcissism and self-referentiality as inescapable
booby traps in any such encounter; and it's about a
human catastrophe, a political problem of global
dimensions. It's also about grief. I hate having to
write what a play is *about*, but I suppose these are
some of the themes of this play.

I didn't imagine, when I was working on the
play, that by the time we produced it the United
States would be at war with Afghanistan. My play is
not a polemic; it was written before September 11,
before we began bombing, and I haven't changed
anything in the play to make it more or less relevant
to current events. It was my feeling when writing the
play that more arrogance, more aggression, more
chaos and more bloodshed were the last things
needed in addressing the desperate situation in
which the Afghan people find themselves. I would
hope my feeling is expressed in the play. It seems to
me that Americans have shown, in recent weeks, a
desire to know much more about Afghanistan. My
greatest hope for a play is always that it might prove
generative of thought, contemplation, discussion—
important components of what I think we want from
our entertainments.

We have been abruptly plunged into horror: by
9/11 first and foremost, by the incomprehensible yet
inescapable fact that we are under attack by an
unknown enemy using biochemical weapons, and by
the actions, both here and abroad, of our own government. More horror is to come. We have been profoundly alienated from our "dailyness," from a certain familiarity and safety without which life
becomes very difficult. It seems to me that one of the

hardest challenges we face is to keep thinking criti-
cally, analytically, compassionately, deeply, even
while angry, mourning, terrified. We need to think
about ourselves, our society—even about our enemies. I have always believed theater can be a useful
part of our collective and individual examining.

Eight months have passed. When we started rehearsing,
the Taliban were still in control of most of Afghanistan;
before the first preview, the Taliban had disappeared. The
American bombing campaign in Afghanistan seems to have
ended the Taliban theocracy, at least for the time being. And
while the Air Force for the most part avoided striking Afghan
cities, there are still no reliable figures for the number of
casualties and fatalities in the current war in Afghanistan. If
the Gulf War is any indication, reliable figures will never
appear. Attempts on the part of the Bush administration to
curtail constitutionally protected freedoms for U.S. citizens,
disinformation campaigns and the like, have met with real
resistance, suggesting a resiliency and enduring vitality
among the watchdogs of our democracy, even in the face of
widespread alarm. The public debate about the legitimacy of
torturing prisoners has gone underground, as has the
anthrax scare and its subsequent investigation. Ground Zero
is now as level as a parking lot. What the U.S. intends for
Afghanistan is anybody's guess. The fate of the people of
Afghanistan is, again, in the hands of the U.S., and there are
ominous signs that we are beginning to lose interest. The
countries responsible for the international force needed to
keep order in the newly destabilized and still heavily armed
country are already showing signs of wanting to withdraw.
And a continued American presence in the region is unlikely
to prove an unmixed blessing. Bush ran for president against
the Clinton administration's record of "nation building."
Hard to know what to make of his present posturing as the
Simón Bolívar of Central Asia; one suspects an oil pipeline

runs through it. His Pontius Pilatism in the occupied territories and his attempt, catastrophically late, to become a peace broker, are rather easier to judge.

The play was written before 9/11. I'm not psychic. If you choose to write about current events there's a good chance you will find the events you've written about to be . . . well, current. If lines in *Homebody/Kabul* seem "eerily prescient" (a phrase repeated so often that my boyfriend Mark suggested I adopt it as a drag name: Eara Lee Prescient) we ought to consider that the information required to foresee, long before 9/11, at least the broad outline of serious trouble ahead was so abundant and easy of access that even a playwright could avail himself of it; and we ought to wonder about the policy, so recently popular with the American right, that whole countries or regions can be cordoned off and summarily tossed out of the international community's considerations, subjected to sanction, and refused assistance by the world's powers, a policy that helped blind our government to geopolitical reality, to say nothing of ethical accountability and moral responsibility.

In addition to the requests to write something after 9/11, I was asked to unwrite something. An editor of a magazine to which I'd contributed a short piece, written before 9/11, emailed to inquire as to whether I would like to remove a sentence in the piece in which I called George W. Bush a "feckless blood-spattered plutocrat" (more executions under his belt than any other governor—any other elected official? —in American history) and Ariel Sharon an "unindicted war criminal" (the Sabra and Shatila massacres in Lebanon). I saw no good reason to make the change. 9/11 may have altered the world forever, and in the process it may have rescued the quasi-legitimate and already-teetering Bush administration, just as it gave new life to the deservedly dashed career of Rudy Giuliani—some of the world's worst people benefited from 9/11—but transformative as the event has proven and will prove to be, nothing changes what has been. The past can't be erased and can only be effaced if we agree to forget, and what has been shouldn't be forgotten. People change, I believe deeply in the possibility of people changing, but Bush? Sharon? Eight months have passed and look at the godforsaken mess the feckless blood-spattered plutocrat and the unindicted war criminal have wrought in the Mideast. Change requires as its catalysts and fuel both good faith and decent intention, as well as deep need. Need, not greed; decent intention, not oil profiteering; good faith, not ethnic cleansing and military occupation cloaked in fundamentalist misreading of Scripture. As Margo Channing reminds us, "Everybody has a heart. Except some people."

If I may be permitted an aside: I know the preceding statement will upset people who believe that the Palestinian Authority, if not the Palestinian people, share equally in the blame for the current nightmare in the Mideast, which threatens the entire planet. I won't concern myself with the fanatics and crazies who believe the Palestinians to be solely responsible. But to the genuinely perplexed, among whose number I count many friends: I am an American and a Jew, and as such I believe I have a direct responsibility for the behavior of Americans and Jews. I deplore suicide bombings and the enemies of the peace process in the Palestinian territories and in the Arab and Muslim world. I deplore equally the brutal and illegal tactics of the IDF in the occupied territories, I deplore the occupation, the forced evacuations, the settlements, the refugee camps, the whole shameful history of the dreadful suffering of the Palestinian people; Jews, of all people, with our history of suffering, should refuse to treat our fellow human beings like that. I deplore the enemies of peace in Israel and in America as well, and to them, inasmuch as they are far more mighty, and already have what the Palestinians seek, statehood, I apportion a greater share of the responsibility for making peace to them. Israel must not be destroyed. The Palestinian State must be established. Peace talks must resume. Sharon must go. Perhaps Arafat should go too, if for no other reason than for the oppressive tactics he employed against his own people before the intifada—but like Sharon he should be removed by the sovereign will of his own people. An international peacekeeping force should take hold of the situation, a condition Israel must accept.

What time in human history is comparable to this? It's nearly impossible to locate plausible occasions for hope. Foulness, corruption, meanness of spirit carry the day. I think a lot about 1939, of the time the Russian writer Victor Serge called "the midnight of the century," when women and men of good conscience, having witnessed the horrors of World War I, watched helplessly, overwhelmed by despair, as fascism and war made their inexorable approaches; as Leninism transformed into Stalinism; a time like this one, when, in Brecht's immortal phrase "there is injustice everywhere/and no rebellion."

Great historical crimes reproduce themselves. One injustice breeds new generations of injustice. Suffering rolls on down through the years, becomes a bleak patrimony, the only inheritance for the disinherited, the key to history, the only certain meaning of life. Sorrow proliferates, evil endures, the only God is the God of Vengeance. Hope dies, the imagination withers and with it the human heart. We no longer dream, not as a people; we are instead demonically possessed. Confronted with the massacre of innocent people, we quibble rather than act; the death of children becomes a regular feature of our daily entertainment. Technology offers oppressor and oppressed alike efficient and cost-effective means of mass murder, and even acts expressive of dissent, defiance and liberation are changed by the appalling progress of weapons development and the global arms market into suicide bombings, into brutal expressions of indiscriminate nihilistic mayhem.

The following speech used to be in the third act of
Homebody/ Kabul, which was, in its first draft, a very long
play. It's still a long play but it used to be longer. This speech,
about Cain, Adam's first son who is according to legend
buried in Kabul, was whittled down to help bring the play
into tighter shape.

Cain was marked, and so they drove him out, everywhere he tried to rest, they drove him away. Only
Kabul did not. He was an extremely old man when
he arrived, many years older than a thousand years
old. Anyone could see that it was past time, that he
was done for, that he could no longer hurt anyone.
His heart was worn out with regretting, after so
many centuries of remorse, it must have been. He
most likely felt nothing at all by the time he arrived
here, an animal looking for a soft bed of leaves,
some place out of the night wind. And this has
always been a hospitable city, welcoming of strangers,
a good host to the weary traveler.

But still it was a great mistake. Letting him stop
here, burying him here. A great mistake.

They should have driven him away.

I was moved by the fact that the city of Kabul was Cain's
resting place. In the play I suggest that he was, perhaps,
murdered there. Over the centuries, so many people have
died in Kabul, in Afghanistan, the number of the slain in the
last four decades perhaps exceeding all those who had fallen
in all the centuries before. Cain was marked not as a sign of
the evil he had committed when he murdered his brother,
but as a protection: God warned the human race to leave the
murderer unharmed. He who killed Cain would be punished
sevenfold. Did Cain die violently in Kabul? Is the city in
some sense cursed? What is the genesis of evil, how far back

does one have to go to find it? Isn't the abandonment of the futile and fatal search for lost causes one place at which a distinction can begin to be made between justice and revenge?

It is in fact only part of the legend that Cain died and was buried in Kabul. The Homebody points out, citing Nancy Hatch Dupree's guidebook, that Cain may have founded the city. This legend has a resonance with the passage in the Holy Scriptures in which we are told that Cain's sons, Jabal, Jubal and Tubalcain, were the human race's first musicians and metalsmiths. There is attached to this destroyer, this hunter, this solitary, desperate, cursed figure of ultimate barrenness, some potential for that renewal of life which is human creativity. Cain is the founder of a city as well as a fratricide, the father of the arts as well as the first person to usurp God's power of determining mortality, the first person to usurp the role of the angel of death.

Tragedy is the annihilation from whence new life springs, the Nothing out of which Something is born. Devastation can be a necessary prelude to a new kind of beauty. Necessary but always bloody. In the preface to his verse drama, *Cain*, Byron tells us: "The world was destroyed several times before the creation of man." That makes a certain sort of sense to me, the history of revolution and modern evolutionary theory lend credence to Byron's breathtaking assertion, but how frightening! Are cataclysm and catastrophe the birth spasms of the future, is the mass grave some sort of cradle, does the future always arrive borne on a torrent of blood?

In my shul, B'Nai Jeshurun, on the High Holy Days, the rabbis prepare a booklet which contains beautiful and provocative passages from the vast body of Jewish spiritual inquiry and explication. And so this year, 5762, days after the towers fell down, the mushroom cloud still visible in the sky over Manhattan, the acrid smoke from the still-burning fires present in every shift in the wind, I read the following sentence, which suggests another kind of prologue to creation, perhaps offers hope for some prelude other than destruction, some other way for the future to commence; from the Talmud (BT Nedarim 39B):

Repentance preceded the world.

Tony Kushner
New York City
April 11, 2002

TONY KUSHNER's plays include *A Bright Room Called Day*, *Angels in America* (Parts One and Two), *Slavs!* and *Hydriotaphia*; as well as adaptations of Corneille's *The Illusion*, Ansky's *The Dybbuk*, Brecht's *The Good Person of Szechuan* and Goethe's *Stella*. Mr. Kushner has been awarded a Pulitzer Prize for Drama, two Tony Awards, the Evening Standard Award, an OBIE, the New York Drama Critics Circle Award, an American Academy of Arts and Letters Award and a Whiting Writers Fellowship, among other awards; recently he received a Lila Wallace/Reader's Digest Fellowship, a medal for Cultural Achievement from the National Foundation for Jewish Culture, the 2002 PEN/Laura Pels Award for Drama and, for *Homebody/Kabul*, The Dramatists Guild Hull-Warriner Award for Best Play. He grew up in Lake Charles, Louisiana, and he lives in New York.